NEIGHBORHOOD NATURALIST:
A WORLD WITHIN WALKING DISTANCE

NAN PENDERGRAST

Photographs of flowers by Britt Pendergrast

Nature's Face Publications

2010

Cover photo: Nan and Britt Pendergrast's back yard full of buttercups

Send comments or corrections to Mark Pendergrast, <u>markp508@gmail.com</u>

Table of Contents

Editor's Note

Neighborhood Naturalist was written by Nan Schwab Pendergrast over several years (primarily between 1980-1985), so that various seasonal occurrences have been conflated into each month. The observations are timeless, however. Every January in Georgia still finds chipmunks scampering through leaves, while picky bluebirds look for an appropriate nesting site. The iris and lilies of the valley remain glorious every April. Poke salad is still a little-appreciated June delicacy, and Nan might prepare some for you on her birthday. (She was born on June 17, 1920.) September brings a hot burst of goldenrod, asters, blazing star, and lobelia, with butterflies dancing attendance. And hawks still soar through the cool December skies, while resurrection fern come magically alive on the oak branches to remind us that spring will eventually return.

I had to do very little editing of this book, in which I can hear my mother's voice so clearly, with her customary passion and curiosity for the world around us. At the end I have added a short appendix of sorts, "Flying in My Mind," written in 2009 as Nan Pendergrast was temporarily kept inside after knee replacement surgery. It records her memories of travel and observations outside of the acres around her Atlanta home that comprise the bulk of *Neighborhood Naturalist*.

--Mark Pendergrast

Nan and Britt Pendergrast

The Beginning

In a suburban neighborhood which, even back in the twenties, was beginning to be encompassed by a burgeoning Atlanta, the lots each measured an acre. The front yards were devoted to monotonous lawns, and the houses themselves were set about with shrubs of Far Eastern origin, purchased from a nurseryman. The space just behind the house was devoted to domestic pursuits -- chicken yards, vegetable patches, and clothes lines adjacent to the spot where fires could be safely set to keep a large pot of clothes simmering on Mondays. Our backyard also had a swing hung from the branch of a large oak, where I could watch the blurred pattern of the leaves against the sky, a pattern that changed with the season and my speed.

Nan Schwab's childhood home on Springdale Road, with the magical back woods

By some tacit agreement, the land at the back of the five yards beyond ours was left alone. In Georgia, land left alone blessedly grows up in trees. This small area was my wilderness. Although it was within reassuring hearing of the rest of the world, so that the chants of the street vendors informing us of "Peachezz, peachezz," or "Strawberreees," or "Iceman" easily penetrated its farthest reaches, I never saw another person there, but I did encounter many creatures. The squirrels, the chipmunks, the birds and the snakes seemed aware that only a skinny girl child ever came there, and that she never chased nor spoke nor sang and often stayed motionless for long moments, simply being.

So a colony of small green snakes slid into and out of their holes near a stream before my gaze. Another larger snake could often be found coiled in a particular patch of sunlight during early spring days, and we looked at each other with interest. It was always I who made the first move. Years later I found a picture of my friend the copperhead in a book about poisonous snakes.

Nan Schwab, the skinny little girl who befriended the squirrels

Glory burst one day when a young squirrel accepted my unspoken invitation and walked trustfully into my outstretched hands. The warmth and the incredibly rapid beat of its heart were against my palms all too briefly before its furious disbelieving mother chattered it away.

The hours spent in this miniature wilderness were the wonderful awakening ones of my childhood. They are far more vivid in my memory than the enforced imprisonment of immobile years in classrooms, more meaningful than the relationships with any people I knew. I think the first strong feeling of rapport with a member of my own species came when I read of Antaeus in a mythology book, and learned of that adversary of Hercules whose strength was renewed whenever he touched the earth.

I went to the woods for understanding and beauty and strength, just as years later my son, harried nearly beyond endurance by the demands of a structured school and society, found solace and serenity where a waterfall tumbled into the small lake on a neighbor's land, where the shores abounded with myriad small creatures, each a vital link in the eternal procession of the days, the years, the centuries, the millennia.

As the seasons came and went, there was a change in my values. It began to be very important that people should like me, and in the tense world of adolescence, I was sure they would not like me if I were not like them. No one I knew cared for wandering about looking at trees and flowers and birds and squirrels, and for a few years neither did I.

Then a life-restoring thing happened. I met Britt, more important than any other person ever could be, and he, of all miracles, liked woods and wild flowers and the wide world of nature. Furthermore, he had a far larger knowledge of the living creatures than I, and a willingness to share my outright idolatry of flowers.

Britt and Nan circa 1939

We were married and, shortly afterward, moved to our bit of wilderness. It was still within the borders of the city of Atlanta, and it, too, actually measured an acre in size. However, although our lot had been dismissed by professional builders as too steep for residential purposes, for us, it was ideal. We felled only the trees in the area where our small house would be built, and virgin oak and hickory towered around us. The land which careened from the house to a small but constant creek and waterfall belonged to our next door neighbor, who cared most diligently for the land immediately surrounding his neat home, and achieved spectacular spring color with azaleas he propagated by air-layering.

He was a generous and gentle man who worried a lot during the thirteen years we lived there. I was fairly constantly pregnant, and he feared that I'd tumble roly-poly down the hill or that one of the five consecutive toddlers would step on a snake or blunder into a nest of yellow jackets.

None of these disasters ever occurred. Slides down the waterfall and breath-taking swings on muscadine vines were survived. We discovered together the first foamflower; its leaves, staying green all the winter, had attracted us and we wondered what spring would bring. It was worth waiting for, the pale pink spire of delicate blossoms, making its scientific name of *Tiarella*, Latin for little crown, seem inevitable. It was one of the many miracles of that first spring, each following the other in dizzying succession.

Foamflower, *Tiarella cordifolio*

My earliest recollection of that house on Springdale Road is that of running to the window in early spring to see if the small bright sun of a dandelion had appeared on the lawn. I remember, too, the adventure of pushing aside the glossy green heart-shaped leaves of wild ginger to find "piggies," the small brown jugs growing at the base. Later, in June, after most of the spring flowers had gone, there was the joy of discovering the tiny lavender bells of the longleaf summer bluet, *Houstonia longifolia*. Above all, I renewed each year the hope embodied in the first small pointed purple bud of a violet.

All the wild flowers meant more to me than their beauty or their fragrance. There was security in the knowledge that every year they came back in the same spots. My first treasures were the pink *Trillium catesbaei* (also known as the bashful wakerobin), whose three petals, nodding below its three leaves, appeared in a special place in the forest of my childhood, and the Solomon's seal with its drooping white bells. I had early sought out books to tell me the names of these friends, and the flowers I found on our hillside with my children were familiar to me already through the pages of the well-worn field guides.

Still, there were surprises, for no books had told me that the sap of the bloodroot is really orange in color, causing me to fret about the probable anemia of the botanist who gave this starry white-flowered member of the poppy family its name. I had never seen the beaked seed pods which gave the wild geranium (*Geranium maculatum*) another title -- cranesbill. Some of the species we found were rare enough to require a dash to the library and consultation with the large reference volumes for identification. My first encounter with a wild orchid, showy orchis, seemed miraculous, and the sudden appearance on the scene of its cousin, the yellow-fringed orchis, in our tenth year of residence, was a mystery I never solved.

Fringed orchis, *Habenaria integra*

Beyond the long-familiar world of the blossoms which starred the forest floor, my joys expanded to include the birds, which had always been melodic blurs to me. Britt's construction and mounting of a tray for birdseed outside the breakfast room window brought the feathered creatures within recognition range of my myopic eyes.

Colors had always been distinguishable to me, so that cardinals and blue jays were old friends, but I had never been able to tell the difference between the cardinal and the tanager, or between the bluebird and the brief brilliant migratory caller, the indigo bunting, until the magic feeding tray was built.

The designs of less spectacular birds -- the crest of the titmouse, the faintly rosy underside of the junco, or snowbird, the two orange-breasted habitues, the towhee and the robin -- were now mine to cherish. Observations of the preferred surroundings of some birds helped me to distinguish between the thrushes who fluttered about in the underbrush, singing their mellow song, and the thrasher, a larger fellow who was more likely to be found in open spaces. The mockingbird and the catbird remain, to this day, confusing to me, unless they are singing, or unless the mocker is courting and spreads his wings to display his proud white feathered wings.

At least one bird, however, was unmistakable, and my first sighting was almost frightening. As I lay on the small porch, savoring Jill's and John's naptime, I suddenly became aware of four huge birds ringing the pine tree only a few feet from the house. Their brilliant red crests and their black and white bodies proclaimed them woodpeckers, as did their assault upon the pine with strong beaks, but they were at least triple the size of the redheaded woodpecker I knew, and their long scrawny necks gave them the look of a creature which should have been extinct for several centuries. When I called Britt at the office to tell of our weird callers, he was able to identify them immediately as pileated woodpeckers.

He was surprised when I told him that they had been silent, and later I came to know well their raucous arrogant cry, which caused country folks to call them Lawd God birds. I witnessed, too, an incident which led me to conclude that their call need not be interpreted as a fierce assertion of territorial rights, but as a warning to other birds or interlopers, or as a message of summons and welcome. My attention was drawn one late summer day by a repeated rackety call, which sounded rather like a bucket of blocks falling downstairs. A pileated woodpecker was swinging acrobatically on a poison ivy vine, vigorously attacking the berries and shouting between lunges. · As I watched, eight or nine smaller birds responded by flying to join the feast.

The woodpecker made no attempt to drive them away, surprising generosity in view of the fact that each one of his species needs five acres of grazing land. Such acreage with the numbers of pines which supply the beetles, his staple diet, have become ever more scarce as they are devoured by bulldozers. Indeed, a close cousin of the pileated woodpecker, the ivory-billed woodpecker, is almost certainly extinct, its last sighting having been reported in Louisiana in 1935. (More recently, in 2004, a Cornell team claimed to have spotted one in Arkansas, but no one ever found it again.) For the present, however, it is a joy to report from personal observation that the pileated woodpecker can not only be seen and heard throughout Georgia, from the mountains in the north to the semi-tropical coasts in the South, but also as far afield from home as Vancouver Island.

Not all the creatures who came to the feeding tray were feathered. Soon the gray squirrels discovered the feast, and we gathered around to admire the snowy whiteness of their undersides and the fluffiness of their tails. We watched and tried to comprehend tail language, for it was clear that they signaled to one another by means of wags. We noticed pretty quickly that the squirrels ate more than their share of the seeds, and that the birds did not dare approach while our furry friends were gorging themselves. At first our lightest tap on the window pane was enough to send them scurrying, but after a few days they learned to ignore this gentle hint that they depart and let some of the other customers have a share. We progressed to opening the window and scratching on the screen, which proved effective for a while, but then we found it necessary to open the screen too and flick the fellows away, and I was uncomfortably aware that they might, if we tried this gambit once too often, turn and snap at us with their sharp teeth.

As we sipped our cups of before-bedtime tea one evening, Britt and I were startled to hear a loud screen-scratching sound. Hurrying to the window, we saw a small brown squirrel with huge dark eyes. Evidently we surprised him too, for he dived from the tray, gliding swiftly and smoothly to the ground some twenty feet below. It was easy to see why he was called a flying squirrel.

These nocturnal visitors to the feeder remained very shy and came rather seldom to feed, so it was a surprise for us to find that they are far more numerous throughout the United States than are their more visible cousins. Britt's brother found that they made delightful pets, after their voracious and noisy chewing in his attic led him to set a Have-a-Heart trap. Several were trapped and released out of doors when they seemed very uneasy in the house, but one settled herself in quickly and became a member of the family, to which she added by giving birth to a litter of very tiny babies.

The infants, too, made themselves at home, sleeping the daylight hours away and, on being released from the cage in the evenings, flying rambunctiously from the curtain rods to the carpets, or snuggling into pockets. When spring came, Brother Bob released the family into the woods surrounding the house, where they were able to provide for their own needs most capably. However, they must have enjoyed the mooching life, for on several occasions they climbed down the chimney into the familiar living room, probably in search of handouts or a cozy pocket. Although they had accepted handling calmly during their months of captivity, they came to object to being hustled out of doors, so that Bob found it necessary to wear thick gloves, else they expressed their displeasure by biting him.

One afternoon I noticed that the tall grass in the lower part of the yard was waving strangely. Investigation disclosed that three very small, but fully furred, opossums were bobbing about there. We did not know it then, but we read up and found that, in spite of their diminutive size, they were several months old, having grown from a birth size equal to that of a honey bee to about the heft of a field mouse. The intervening days had been spent snug in their mother's pouch. When they were mature enough to venture outside, they still stayed close to their mother, either clinging to her long hair or wrapping their bare rat-like tails around hers. How these three had gone wandering we never knew, but it is doubtful that their parent, who had given birth to a litter of fifteen or so, had missed them.

Opossums will eat almost anything they can get, whether fruit, eggs, vegetables, or carrion, and I've been told that they themselves taste rather like greasy pork. I have never sampled their meat, nor had the faintest desire to do so, ever since I once mistook a skinned opossum carcass, hanging from a laundry line near a country shack on a crisp autumn day, for a human infant. Myopia leads to strange terrors now and then. We took our orphans to a children's zoo.

There was one occasion when Britt and I had cause to wonder if we might not have overdone the fondness for all living creatures. Britt called me to show me a thick husky copperhead snake near the gate to our small cleared yard. In the summer dusk, I had trouble finding it, as it lay still, even as Britt approached it with a hoe. When we were assured that the snake was quite dead, we called Jill and John, who were then about four and two, to come and see the new discovery. "What," I asked, "would you do if you were out walking and saw a snake like this?" Jill was prompt with her response. "I'd pat it," she said, but John said forcefully, "No. No, Jill! I'd step on it!" We spent a while studying pictures of snakes in the reptile book and ended by advising that they depart swiftly from any snake they saw.

Later we learned that, while it is still sensible to step aside from copperheads, their bite is not fatal. It does occasion several very miserable days, however. The two people we knew who were bitten had actually reached out inadvertently and made contact with the snake, one walking along a concrete path to his city home in the summer twilight. He never actually saw the creature that bit him on the ankle, but he thought it a sting of some sort, which he mentioned casually to his family. Within minutes, however, the reaction was violent, and he was rushed to the hospital. The other, alone at the home of a neighbor deep in the woods, was clearing brush when he reached into the wrong spot and was bitten on the hand. He did not realize the seriousness of the situation, so that when his employer came home two hours later, he was semi-conscious, with a hugely swollen arm. Even with the delayed treatment, he recovered.

Copperhead camouflage is excellent, so that I weeded a patch in our flower bed for almost an hour before I noticed a copperhead coiled in a clump of iris about three feet away. He must have been there observing or dozing the whole time, for I would surely have noticed his approach. It is fortunate that they are not in the least aggressive, for they seem fond of being close to people. One inexplicably showed up in the front hall of Britt's mother's home, and we have found seven where we live now.

To return to the early days on Putnam Circle, the thirteen years we lived in the little house in the woods were years of discovery for all of us. Our findings were multiplied in value through being shared with very young children.

Nan in front of Putnam Circle home; Britt with John, looking at birds

It was not at all a matter of our pointing out new sights and sounds to our offspring. Far more often the treasures were sighted or heard by the newer eyes and ears, observed by those whose minds were uncluttered by grocery lists and loathing of McCarthyism.

At first motion and color were enough to attract their attention, the play of colors on the splendid roundness of a soap bubble, the motes floating in a ray of sunlight. Somewhat later, by about the age of three, questions began to come with rapidity and variety. Why does the spider spin his web? Why can't we see stars in the daytime? How do seeds grow? It was reassuring to find that my inability to supply an instant answer was far less important than my willingness to drop everything and try to seek it out.

There are times when it is necessary to know a bit about a subject in order to ask about it. Any child can find humor in a hopping frog, but when one also knows something about the life history of the amphibian — from the minute egg on the surface of the pond, its topside black to absorb the heat of the sun's rays to speed hatching, the underside white for camouflage from predators below, then the change to wiggling tadpole, and finally this leaping fellow — a true wonder has been found.

Every child loves happy endings and we had no need to look further than the nearest caterpillar to find one, for a fairy tale was commencing before our eyes. Its climax, of course, came when the magnificent butterfly emerged from its cocoon.

Each of us seems to be born with a taste for serious drama as well, including stark tragedy, so long as it does not affect us personally. To be aware of the struggle of very small creatures for survival involves us in the trickery of the spider, which can be disguised as a fluff of thread or a seed, or the lethal hide-and-seek of the chameleon and the praying mantis, and a thousand other plots compared to which the mindless and repetitious violence of television pales into mediocrity.

Walking at the pace of a two-year-old leads to findings which would never be observed at an adult speed. It was five-year-old Scott who pointed out to me that the stream had many levels -- the surface where the waterbugs skittered, the water itself where the minnows swam among the currents of the small rapids formed by the pebbles, and the sand beneath, where the oversized circular shadows of the waterbugs' feet formed constantly shifting patterns. We found that there was yet another level when we lifted a larger rock from the sand and found a crayfish beneath. I have never since seen a stream on a single level.

Time was when I overreacted to what I regarded as insect damage, so that I bought some stuff of nauseating odor called SCOPE to eradicate leaf miners, microscopic creatures who nibble at the innards of boxwood foliage. Now I know that helpful bugs outnumber those that are harmful, from the human point of view, by ten to one. The insecticide did not really seem to have all that much impact on the leaf miners, so that I stopped using SCOPE even before I gained enough sense to eschew all pesticides. The boxwood have survived well, and the cardinal, deep in winter when other food is less available, seems grateful for a feast of miner eggs. Chickadees fancy them as well.

The most cherished insect for us is the honeybee, and we are hardly alone in our interest and affection for him. The widest literature in the world, next to that of man and his affairs, deals with this insect. From the earliest days philosophers, scientists and just plain observers have written of the life of the bee. This is not surprising, for the life of the bee is one of the abiding marvels, an extraordinary civilization much older than ours. In addition, people have been fascinated by the bee as the source of extraordinary sweetness. Its importance is indicated by the many mentions in the Bible of honey as the epitome of all that is good, but its real worth was perhaps best and earliest delineated in the epitaph written for himself by an ancient Babylonian governor, Shamashresh-usur, who hoped to be remembered as the man "who brought down bees from the mountains of the Khabkha tribe, and I put them in the garden of Gabari-ibni. They collected honey and wax."

It was our son Scott who brought bees home, a hive full of them, and we established them at the foot of the hill in the backwoods. We had been told this was an ideal location, since they could leave the hive and fly uphill while they were unburdened, then coast down when laden with pollen. They made themselves right at home, but trouble came when we brought home wild honey robbed from bees who had taken over the entire wall of an old house in the country. Our bees rushed in for their share of the harvest, and when spring came, we discovered that our hive was empty of bees, and unfortunately full of the larvae of the wax moth, which moves into an empty hive to feast on wax. We are not certain what happened, but think it likely that the wild honey contained foulbrood, a dread disease which destroys an entire hive.

By this time Scott had heard a whitewater river call irresistibly, and we were left with the defunct hive and a decision. Although most of the authorities we consulted recommended the destruction of a hive that had been inhabited by wax moth larvae, Britt thriftily searched until he found one who held out hope for re-use if the hive were boiled in water containing caustic soda, so the old washpot, idle since the clothes-boiling days of my childhood, was hauled out and put to work.

When we installed a colony, complete with queen, we were at last on our way to being honey harvesters on our own place. Our hives produced about three gallons each, and there are now two, since we were able to divide the colony. On at least one occasion, we were not alert to the crowded conditions and found out only when thousands swarmed, forming a large black buzzing ball high in a pine tree, before they flew away to set up housekeeping elsewhere.

Robbing the hive is an adventure, and one for which I stand at a safe distance. Britt, wearing as sting-proof an outfit as we can devise, takes a bellows and smokes the hive, a process which I would have thought would make them highly irritable. However, the smoke diverts them from the thief in their midst, for they become totally occupied with protecting their honey from fire. Our honey, rich and dark brown, is gathered from many floral sources, and gives me a reason beyond self-indulgence to try to grow many varieties of flowers. It has been a surprise to me that they do not seem to prefer bright and large flowers, but instead especially favor the small greenish flowers of the holly bushes and the pale yellow bell-shaped flowers which occur in clusters on the mahonia, perhaps because it is the first flower to appear in the new spring season. I would never have bought the plant for landscaping purposes, for its prickly leaves are vicious, and its method of growth is stiff and awkward. It is an evergreen, however, and when I discovered that the birds had brought some into the forest, I moved several out to see what a touch of sun would do. They quickly expressed their appreciation for the light and more space by growing quickly and putting forth blossoms.

In early January, lured by the wintry sun, the bees venture out, first for tentative flights, flying in small circles near their doorway and re-entering the dark warmth fairly frequently. Some braver souls among them fly uphill to search out the mahonia, and when I first see them there, I feel that the year has properly begun.

The arrival of our sixth child crowded us out of our first beloved house. We had long before changed what had originally been a breakfast room to a nursery, had added a bedroom downstairs, and in one extremely nervous construction feat, spent several nights roofless while we tacked on a second story, but there was simply nowhere to put the newest son.

It was fortunate that we found another house on a hill on West Paces Ferry Road, with land four times the acreage of our first dwelling.

Our second (and final) home on West Paces Ferry Road

There were many advantages, including enough floor space so that I need no longer spend my days ineffectually trying to shush the natural happy noises of children at play for fear of waking a sleeping infant. The house was five years old when we bought it, and although we would never have cleared so much space around it, we found that sunlight did allow us to indulge in the zinnias and larkspur and petunias that had never thrived in our shaded space.

On the other hand, we mourned our lost lush woods and the stream and waterfall. Our new lot was varied in its vegetation, with the front north slope nearly barren. The construction of the house and the driveway had pretty well destroyed many of the trees, and it was depressing to watch the puny pine seedlings and the raw red bank by the street.

Yet the steeper slope behind us had not been disturbed, sheltering holly and a pawpaw patch and magnolia seedlings that kept their green all year long, beneath larger oaks and hickories as well as the colorful dogwood and sourwood. Beyond, at the very back of our land, was a level space where the furrows of a farm field planted a century ago were still faintly discernible. When agricultural activities were abandoned, pines grew, attaining great heights and diameters of up to three feet. There were, when we moved here thirty-five years ago, relatively few wild flowers, except for a few welcome hepaticas, some pink trillium, and wood violets.

Pink trillium, *Trillium catesbei*

If we had no water on our own place, or even immediately adjacent to it, there were consolations. Nancy Creek flowed nearby, and a two-mile walk brought us to the shores of the Chattahoochee River. Our neighbors had left their woods undisturbed, and they have shown total permissiveness to my wanderings.

The land, the plants that grow on it, and the wild creatures who inhabit it, are far more adaptable and resilient than I dreamed. Beyond waging a continuous war on greenbrier and honeysuckle, we have left the woods alone, and wondrous newcomers, brought by the wind or the birds, have arrived to take up residence, to thrive and to multiply. Each year, I notice new trees, maples and viburnum, beech and sassafras, to name a very few.

Constant discoveries are a part of walking the same land through thirty springs, summers, falls, and winters, the ever-recurring yet ever-new life around us. Each year brings me a deeper appreciation of what I've observed, along with increased awareness of how little I know. The journal that follows records a year of life for us.

Nan Pendergrast gathering wildflowers in 1981

January

Of early January in Georgia, Stephen Vincent Benet wrote:

The little New Year, the weakling one,
Can lie outdoors in the noonday sun,
Blowing the fluff from a turkey-wing
At skies already haunted with Spring.

He is often right, and many a New Year's Day here in Atlanta we have seen the bluebirds flying about, inspecting each of the four houses Britt has constructed to their exacting specifications. Of course there are no birds quite so indecisive as bluebirds, whether the parents are choosing a lodging or the young are trying to make up their minds to leave the nest after the earlier decision has finally been made.

The chipmunks, who go into a brief semi-hibernation in winter here, are often scampering through the leaves, searching for overlooked hickory nuts or acorns, and the flowering quince may have burst into blossom, luring the bees to browse.

Yet January can be an unpredictable hussy, so that we are grateful that the vegetable seeds we sowed a few days earlier in the cold frame have not yet sprouted. The frames, which afford us a chance to give spinach and broccoli a head start, are the inadvertent gifts of neighbors. The bricks that form their low walls were donated by a fellow down the street who discarded some slightly broken ones when his house was being built. The plastic shielding the seedlings from the cold was found encasing the leaves other neighbors industriously raked, stuffed into sacks and deposited by the street. Most important, the rich dark soil nurturing the plants was the product of the leaves from year before last. The frames on which the erstwhile plastic bags were stretched once surrounded window screens discarded by yet another profligate fellow from around the block. It very seldom gets cold enough to penetrate the covering, and we usually are feasting on spinach salads by March.

There was, however, one unforgettable January when three inches of snow were overlaid by frozen rain, turning our world into a crystalline fairyland, where every twig sparkled in the bright sunlight that followed. All seemed unfamiliar as the contours of the land were accentuated by the white coverlet. There were hummocks my feet had never before noticed, but then perhaps never before had my feet moved so consciously and warily. It was a challenge to descend the hills, and the wet-weather creek that I had mistaken for a Confederate trench meandered visibly through the slopes. It was plain that it would indeed have been, as a historian friend pointed out, a damned stupid place for a trench.

A seeker of artifacts of the "Late Unpleasantness," as my grandparents used to speak of the Civil War of 1861-65, he had brought his metal detector to explore the backwoods, and he hazarded a guess that, if

16

there had indeed been soldiers here over a century ago, they would have been up on the ridge. So saying, he had marched up there himself and almost immediately unearthed a small cache of minie balls. They were, he determined from their three rings, unfired Yankee bullets, either dropped in haste, or perhaps because the soldier who carried them was tired of their weight.   It was amazing that, after so long a time of lying undisturbed, the bullets were so close to the surface. It was evident that the years of falling leaves had been blown away by the years of winter winds, and the soil had built up very slowly.

Daffodils in bloom a bit later

Only a few days later, more normal January weather had set in, and the daffodil spikes pierced the ground, while the hellebore, or Christmas rose, was ready to burst into bloom. No native plant this, but an exotic cousin of the peony, which I had discovered flowering on a trash heap on a vacant lot and hauled home. Now it is surrounded by literally hundreds of seedlings, which grow very slowly. Several of them finally flowered in their third year, and I discovered that they do not breed true in color, so that the pinkish parent has produced some offspring with pale green blossoms.

Hellebore, *Helleborus niger,* **or Christmas rose**

The spinach seedlings must generate their own heat, for during the snowiest of the days, each small plant had melted the area immediately surrounding it, and its glossy green leaves showed us that all was not lost.

There have been January days, too, when every contour was obliterated by thick fog. With the temperature in the sixties, there was nothing to be seen at a distance of more than two feet. The dogs and I then tramp through a mysterious landscape, where even the trees we know so well loomed strange and startling.

When the weather suddenly turned seasonably chill, the wood stove proved itself a wondrous addition to our lives, a source of even, moist warmth that has kept plants in the house happier longer than gas heat has ever done. This gentle heat also failed to tarnish silver, and, given its own sweet time, could fry a great egg. I found that its versatility was almost boundless, for while it warmed three rooms, it cooked dinner and dried towels. On the coldest nights, it obligingly heated the bricks that we wrapped in soft cloth and whisked upstairs to the frigid bedroom and slipped under the sheets to spread comfort -- ah, luxury!

Even at its coldest, Georgia January exhibited hints that spring was not all that far distant. Along the western palisades bordering the river, green was everywhere. The rhododendron and the mountain laurel were fully clothed in shining leaves, and the rounded buds of the former and the spiky ones of the latter indicated clearly that flowering season was just around the corner. The leaves of the leucothoe and those of the galax had turned deepest red in the cold, as had some of the hepatica's three-lobed foliage. The shiny black salamanders had awakened with breeding on their minds.

Clitoria ternatea

February

The shortest month began with a torrential rainfall. During the night, I heard it pelting onto the roof and gushing down the gutterspouts. The following morning a watery sun appeared, and, as I sloshed along familiar paths, I found that little gullies had become small streams. As I followed them to Nancy Creek, I found that it had become a torrent. Rushing water tumbled over roots and rocks, splashing and gurgling where I had never heard it before. The trees, bared except for their clumps of mistletoe, formed the backdrop for the color of an extraordinarily large and varied group of birds -- noisy brilliant jays, cardinals and redheaded woodpeckers. I saw the white flash of the mockingbird's wings, and down by the swollen river, a flock of cedar waxwings, early trippers toward the north who had stopped to gorge themselves on the ligustrum berries. Spring peepers were chirtling (and if there is no such word, there ought to be), their chorus seeming to vibrate the bog.

There are many resemblances in nature, and the visual ones have often puzzled me. At some distance, it is hard for me to tell whether the brown creature bustling about in the leaves is a sparrow or a chipmunk until it walks or flies, as the case may be. But I'd always thought the sounds of the out of doors were individual and quite unmistakable, given a familiarity with the source. A few days after the big rain, I was puzzled by a sound that seemed exactly like the bubbling of the swift-flowing streams, and yet there was no water flowing anywhere near, and the lovely sound emanated from a small group of magnolia trees, a melodious cascade of song from a few redwinged blackbirds. I had never heard them sing like that, but now I've learned that, like their cousins the blue jays, they have the capacity to create beautiful sounds, but do not often indulge. I would never have suspected that streams and blackbirds have sounds in common, but I recognized with joy that I have a lot to learn.

A week or so later, I observed an unusual number of birds feeding in the back yard. There were two thrashers, three flickers, nine robins, a towhee or two, the usual clutch of jays, and a cardinal couple. Seldom did all come at once, particularly when I had scattered no seed for them recently. They stood in a wavering sort of line, quite still, and at first I was bewildered, but when I looked more carefully, I understood.

The weather had been exceptionally warm for the past day, and it was evident that the angleworms, who move deep underground to avoid the chill of wintry soil, had come closer to the surface to savor the more comfortable surroundings. They had, in turn, been followed upward by their soft furry predators, the moles. These sturdy little mammals require a considerable number of insects, and worms and grubs are their favorite delicacies. They spend the better part of their lives burrowing with their hard noses and amazingly strong and agile claws in search of food.

The birds, of course, share the moles' fondness for gourmet grubs and worms, so they were following the tunnel's course above ground in search of leftovers. The moles had done a thorough job of stirring up the soil, and the feathered fellows were all pecking so vigorously that they seemed to have no interest in defending their territory. When a pair of redheaded woodpeckers flew in to join the feast, they simply settled in on an untended length of tunnel, rather than assert pecking order by routing the jays, as I had often seen them do.

For the sake of loamy, well-aerated soil, I hoped that there were a plentiful supply of worms left for the tender roots of spinach, broccoli, and chard. Occasionally moles have aerated entirely too well and inadvertently killed some strawberry plants. Someone told us that children's toy windmills poked into the ground would revolve in the breeze, setting up a vibration that would frighten the moles away. The toys made a colorful addition to the garden, pleasant to watch, but the moles were utterly undeterred. This year we will try another suggested method for discouraging moles -- sprinkling cayenne pepper near the strawberry bed. Gardeners are, in the nature of the breed, ever and unreasonably hopeful.

Speaking of aerated soil, it seems to come as a terrible shock to transplanted Midwesterners when they come, trowel in hand, to begin to take advantage of our early spring planting season. If it has been dry, they find the soil virtually impenetrable. If, on the other hand, it has been a typically wet February, they find that the trowel will enter with no problem but seems reluctant to emerge. They discover that what we have beneath the luxuriant growth of weeds is red clay, different in color and consistency from anything they had encountered in Ohio, Indiana, or Iowa.

Many newcomers are inclined to give the whole idea of Georgia gardening a miss, and it is true that the clay needs rich black compost added. When we discovered how quickly leaves rotted to form compost, we overdid its use, indulging ourselves in raised beds from which we had carefully removed every trace of the red stuff. It was rich all right, but so loose that the roots tended to come up whenever it rained or blew, and the plants ran largely to impressive foliage and small fruit.

The encyclopedia told us that soil is the portion of the earth's surface in which it is possible for plants to grow. It is made up of mineral and organic matter, and the red clay, made up of rock which has been broken down by weathering, may be difficult to work with, but it is also essential to the growth of plants. Its extremely small particles do not allow the necessary air to reach the plants' roots, so we have found that the proper recipe for us is to mix the clay about half and half with compost.

When a wind of near-tornado force blew through some while ago, it uprooted huge oaks, so that we could see that their roots had been embedded in the reddest, most unadulterated clay, and only a thin layer of black topsoil had provided the organic nourishment needed to grow the giants. We have watched with interest to see how long it will take for something to sprout in the cavities, and what type of plants they will be. As I write, two months after the big blow, there is not yet a sprout of any sort.

The wild creatures who share our turf and skies are usually quite small, ranging from insects to ravenous shrews and the black salamander uncovered when rocks were moved in the creek. About the largest native creature I'd seen around here was the muskrat, so it was astonishing to be told that a turtle many times that size lived in the beaver pond. I have not seen the fifty-pound snapping turtle myself, but I have faith in the witness to its residence. He is a fellow who has done a lot of fishing in the pond, and he did show me a three-foot long catfish he had hauled from its depths.

The beaver pond dam is humbling to see. I have yet to see the architects, but these energetic furred engineers have provided a swamp where wood duck live, and they have drowned the fences which people built to mark now meaningless boundaries. The gnawed stumps on the shore bear mute witness to the beavers' work, and, though I know the pond itself to be relatively new, there is already a primeval look about the place. It is an area in change, where each year more aquatic plants grow, and more crayfish mounds appear.

Trout lily, *Erythronium americanum*

By midmonth, there were subtle signs that spring was almost here, although a casual glance could only note the lack of flowers or fresh greenery. But there was a different spirit moving the squirrels, who alternated eating the scattered seeds with periods of pure play, when they romped, chased one another over and occasionally under the fallen logs, and scampered up the small trees, flaunting their semaphoric bushy tails. After they finally tired and retreated to their leafy homes in the tall trees, the birds came to breakfast. In the vanguard were gentle doves with their smooth unhurried steps, in contrast to the frantic scratching of the towhee, or ground robin, making last fall's leaves fly beneath the bushes.

Inspired by all this activity, I ventured into the woods and was rewarded by the discovery of the first small shoots of the trout lily piercing the earth, and the first lacy leaves of the dentaria. If I'd had a bushy tail, I'd have whisked it in sheer delight, for spring was clearly coming.

And yet, and yet, a week or so later, as February was drawing to a close, I was reminded what a heartbreaker this month could be. There was a sudden freeze, and the daffodils, which had been lured by warmth into full flower, were bent by a wind in the teens blustering out of the north. I cut them quickly, and brought them into the house, where the lovely warmth of the wood stove revived them miraculously.

As the month neared its end, there were a few pink camellias on sheltered inner branches of the bush, solace for those that had flowered earlier and been hit by a freeze. The crocus blossomed, purple and golden cups of beauty.

Crocus

And I noticed for the first time a mist of blue by the roadside, which, on close inspection turned out to be hundreds of very small flowers, known as star violets, or *Houstonia minima*. Had they been there every February, and had I simply failed to see?

Looking up, I saw more signs of coming spring. The red maple was in full flower and a bunch of catkins drooped from the alder by the stream. In drier woods, the first new leaves appeared in the elder, reminding me that I promised myself several years back to try making jelly from the berries, if the birds were not swifter at the harvest. The buckeye was budding fat, and the birds went about the business of planning families.

Red buckeye, *Aesculus pavia*

Doves pursued each other through the bare woods, and we heard the cardinal call in his most piercing voice before the sun was up. The towhees had made plans to nest in the boxwood by the back door, perching there and repeating their name whenever we passed.

We made a tasty discovery when new green leaves appeared in the vegetable beds, and then, still deep in winter, the plants put forth buds and delicate white flowers. They turned out to be cardamine cress, delicious, slightly less tangy cousins of the watercress that once grew in a stream nearby, before disappearing when construction clogged the waters with clay. It was good to find a replacement, though we did not know whether to thank birds or breezes for its appearance.

Beginning in 2005, Friendly the fawn came to visit the Pendergrast back woods (and yard) regularly with her mother.

March

March has always been the most unpredictable of months. Whenever the first touch of spring came, I was persuaded that the cold was gone. Occasionally this delusion led to physical downfall. When I walked to the neighboring school one early March morning to tutor, I was so enthralled by the patterns of red maple in flower against the backdrop of a startlingly blue sky that I failed to look where my feet were going. I slipped and fell flat in a patch of ice.

It was a blunt reminder that winter was still here, according to the calendar, although the brilliant gold of dandelions, daffodils, forsythia, and jasmine did their best to persuade me otherwise.

Carolina jasmine

Speaking of dandelions, it has always puzzled me that the flower's name is a corruption of the French *dents de lion*, or lion's teeth. It looks far more like a small sun, or bright coin.

If there have been disappointments and bumps in March, there have always been compensations, too. The leafless trees of March preside over a succession of flowers on the forest floor. Taking advantage of the increasing warmth and the unusual sunlight on their patch of ground, the hepaticas bloom, erupting from their fuzzy buds and displaying their bright blue faces, The bloodroot, starry white against last fall's brown leaves, appears next to the trout lilies, whose buds nod before the yellow petals open and bend backward to show the maroon stamens.

Bloodroot, *Sanguinaria canadensis*

Both the hepatica and the trout lilies were brought into our woods as part of a rescue mission. In fact, it has often occurred to me that our gardens, totally devoid of design, are more of a plant refuge than anything else. The hepatica were transplanted from a tract when their ultimate doom was foreshadowed by a sign proclaiming that it had been rezoned for commercial development. Since there were a few of their species here as natives on our land, I did not have much fear that the move would disturb them.

The trout lilies were another matter. I had found them growing only at streamsides and in bogs. So when I discovered that a patch growing on a creek bank was threatened by imminent construction of a bridge, I worried about transplanting them to our hillside, far above any stream or creek. Since their destruction was inevitable, I dug them up and brought them home anyway. I watched anxiously to see if they could survive in an unusual habitat. Not only did they survive, but multiplied, and I was emboldened to bring may apples, which my children always called umbrella plants because of the double large leaves hiding the white blossom beneath.

Plants, we have found, are far more likely to adapt to a drier environment than to a wetter one, where they have tended to rot. Of course, when we have had extremely dry summers, we've made sure that these refugees have had their share of sprinkling. We've discovered, too, that when it has been necessary to move a plant at what would seem to be an improper time of year, as bulldozers threatened, the move has been successful more often than not, as long as we have taken enough soil so that the roots were only minimally disturbed, and so long as we remembered that even the most careful of transplants is equivalent to surgery, and recuperation must be furthered with frequent watering for at least several weeks.

Some plants, of course, were far more difficult than others. When the widening of the highway meant destruction to the pink azalea whose fragrance and beauty had enlivened our route to the nearby shopping center, we knew that at least a part of their shallow but widespread root system would have to be sacrificed, and that, without downright brutal pruning, it would be a decade before it would flower again.

So far as we can tell, most members of the orchid family are virtually immovable, although we have been able to keep lady's slippers for several years before they begin to diminish and ultimately disappear.

There have been a few failures, but the successes of the rescue missions have far outnumbered them, and the memories of once-beautiful places and departed friends have come afresh with many springs, and often we have been able to share the seedlings with others. Thus, the blue phlox has always reminded me of its donor, Happy, who settled back in her native Long Island. The crabapple trees, offering banquets of sweetness to the honeybees, were also a gift from her.

Anemone quinquefolia

But, in moving on to crabapples, I am getting a long way ahead of recollections of early Marches, when the glories at hand include the pale pink buds of the apparently delicate rue anemone, whose wiry stems bend resiliently in the brisk winds, straightening again to display the white flowers. Its name means "wind" in Greek.

In the woods, now quite naturalized and innumerable, danced the small daffodils, all descendants of a dozen brought in many years ago when the field in which they grew was about to be buried beneath the vast concrete gravestone of a parking lot.

Although the March temperature sometimes dips below freezing on several nights, the windy sunny days are usually brisk and challenging, and the flowers seem undisturbed by the cold dark hours of the night.

March has always been particularly fortuitous for getting better acquainted with birds. For one thing, they are very noticeable among the not-yet-leafed-out trees, and already courtship is under way and nesting materials being gathered. Sometimes, the nesting places they choose make it clear why "birdbrained" does not mean intelligent. The wrens, for instance, perky, melodic, very welcome visitors hereabouts, chose last March to construct their nest in the downspout of the gutter by the front door, a location sure to result in disastrous flooding with the first rain. We wondered whether to incur the risk of their lasting distrust by destroying the nest before there were any eggs to be lost, or stand aside and let nature do its worst to their family. However, we and the wrens were lucky, as a painful decision was avoided. During the critical period, no rain fell.

At this season, too, a reason to pay close attention to birds is that they usually, with their minds much on romance and home-building, pay little attention to us. I very nearly stumbled over a flicker pecking at the roots of an oak near Nancy Creek, and he did not bother to fly away. There was so much to see on and by the creek itself that I had not noticed him either.

It has been encouraging to see the changes that have occurred there since our first meeting, when the water was constantly brown and sluggish, and there was no sign of aquatic life. Too many houses had been constructed on its banks upstream, and too many tons of Georgia's red clay had been washed into it.

Gradually, however, over the years, the situation has improved. I'm not sure why, but possibly all the building sites have been used. So far as I know, no legislation was passed to protect its waters, and yet a few years back, I saw the first fish, and shortly afterward, the kingfishers came, coursing and occasionally diving. One memorable day, just as I started to cross the bridge, two ducks virtually exploded from beneath, making such a swift and audibly whirring departure that I had only a glimpse of them.

Within my walking radius of four miles or so, there are three accesses to the Chattahoochee River, and each brings me to a different world of plants and birds and creatures. The morning mist rises slowly, disclosing the wide waters flowing very slowly toward the Gulf of Mexico. We have been to see the headwaters of this river of the painted rocks, as the Indians called it, a small sparklingly clear mountain stream about 100 miles to the north, and we have paddled canoes in the river after it has been swollen by countless nameless tributaries, at the remains of old Jones Bridge and below the old dam. It is not a navigable river for craft large enough to carry commercial quantities of anything when it reaches our neighborhood, and we are selfishly grateful. Except for a relatively small stretch of water infested with beer-can-tossing rafters, its length is left to the beaver, muskrat, herons and kingfishers, and to us.

We once saw a quartet of black vultures perched high in a dead pine, who took turns cruising the river, never, so far as we could see, finding any prey. We returned the following day and found them in the same place. After that, they departed. Their 57-inch wing span is impressive.

The river is home year-round to mallards, and to an ever-increasing mob of Canada geese. Very occasionally, coots fly in, and trim black-and-white buffleheads call annually, as do hooded mergansers.

The great blue herons are also year-round residents, welcome on the river, less so by owners of costly koi fishponds, which they seem to have an unerring instinct to discover for feasting.

Of course, the river's inhabitants change from season to season, and there was one memorable year when a long-lasting drought forced animals which usually do not come within many miles of the city to follow the course of the Chattahoochee in search of food. A brown bear was found on a golf course closer to the center of town than we. Its discovery caused Britt to eat a few skeptical words he had spoken when one of our neighbors claimed to have smelled a bear in his woods a day or so before. His St. Bernard had roused him late one night, barking ferociously but apparently too frightened to venture out of doors. His master stepped to open the door and sniffed the unmistakable scent of bear, with which he, a hunter, claimed to be familiar. There were many hoots of derision at the gathering when he told of this incident, and some apologies later.

A voyage down the river one day took us past the Palisades on an unusually balmy March night, lighted by a full moon. The scene was at once familiar and totally unknown; for the same rocky cliffs of the Palisades section of the Chattahoochee rose sharply on the southern shore, but the tracery of the bare limbs of the trees was silhouetted against the night sky, the clumps of mistletoe seeming to accentuate the clean lines of the strange sight of the leafless trees.

The rocks, too, rising out of the water, differed in shape. There were lumps, one or two on almost every rock. When we approached silently in the canoe, they stayed immobile until we were right upon them, then dived into the water. If the creature slipped without a sound into the river, we knew it was a muskrat. If there was instead, a violent splashing that sprinkled us thoroughly, we knew that we had disturbed a beaver, who had slapped his flat tail in a signal of alarm.

Of course, we had seen the muskrats occasionally swimming in the river at dusk, and we knew from the gnawed stumps of river birches on the shore that beaver were in residence in the area, but I had never, until the moonlight helped, so much as glimpsed them. A neighbor whose home is on the shore downstream from where we paddled had told me of seeing the beaver family, mama and papa trailed by their young, making a trip down the side of the tributary where their dam had created a pond. She was aware of their habitation and at first was worried that the trees they gnawed down and used in their construction project might eventually denude the shore. However, a Department of Agriculture expert reassured her that they tended to fell only small or gnarled trees, and would probably, in the long run, benefit the forest by their culling.

Each March has seemed to bring new discoveries. The blossoming of the first woodland flowers has always been so entrancing that I have sought out the places where I've learned to look for them, adoring their beauty and being grateful for the security afforded by the knowledge that, where man has left them undisturbed, they will return year after year.

Along with recurrent marvels have come new observations. The birds, I've found, are silent in March. The mockingbird traverses the fields at the school, raising and lowering his tail as rhythmically as a metronome. Why? The wrens forage quietly among the bushes bordering the field, and the robins are intent on learning and listening.

Annually during this month, I visit a familiar cliff to welcome the attractively mottled leaves of the toad trillium. It is one of spring's first arrivals, forming a frame for the maroon, three-petaled flower that always seems to be on the verge of opening wide, but never does. I've learned to look, too, for the dentaria's pink bells. Only recently did I really look at the cliffs above, and there, among the rocks, were the fragile flowers of the early saxifrage. The name, meaning "stone breaker," describes the plant's preferred habitat, and led to the use of a potion made from its leaves to dissolve kidney stones. Unfortunately it was ineffective.

How could I have failed to note before now that honeybees are very fond of dandelions? After remarking on the birds' silence, I saw for the first time an activity about which I'd read. A pair of doves were cooing, a soothing sound likely to be heard any month of the year when the day happens to be mild, but these were also engaged in billing. They were perched on a telephone wire, oblivious, in their courtship, of a gaggle of garden club ladies chattering directly beneath. The birds were pecking at each other ever so gently with their bills, then preening the iridescent feathers of the beloved's neck. Then they kissed, deeply and at length, a romantic and moving sight for me. Later I read that during the osculation, they often exchange regurgitation. Somehow this would not turn me on, but to each species its own titivation.

April

The fascination of the observation of nature lies not only in its beauty and drama, but in its infinite variety. A slight change in climate, an excessive or diminished amount of rainfall, the errant flight of a bird, a shift in wind pattern, can and do make of each spring a new adventure.

During the past year, the weather has been cooler for far longer than usual, and as a result the lilacs, which have a habit here in the South of flowering and fading very quickly, with blossoms pale and almost without fragrance, have this year produced heavy plumes of deep lavender, with a bouquet which caresses the nose as soon as we step out of the back door. The colors of many of the flowers seem brighter and the foliage larger, so that the lilies of the valley are startlingly white against their deep green leaves, last longer, and smell sweeter, while the bluebells, both the *Mertensia* and the English wood hyacinth, are the color of an October sky. The sprays of the bleeding heart are fuller, and the iris extraordinarily glorious.

Crested iris, *Iris cristata*

Because it has also rained harder and longer this spring, Nancy Creek spilled over its banks into the little lakes nearby. The waters brought to delicious life morels that popped up overnight in a boggy area where they had not appeared during my three decades of watching. How did they get there? It would be hard to find out, for the spores are so light that they float with ease on the air currents above the ocean, wafting to us the same delicate mushroom which has long been the object of hunts through the French and Belgian woodlands in spring. It is a distinctively shaped and therefore easily recognizable fungus and its flavor is worth the hunting.

Here in our Georgia woods or fields, mushrooms are likely to spring up in any month of the year when there has been a fairly lengthy spell of rainy weather. They are paradoxical plants, for the small buttons appear suddenly, becoming small umbrellas the following day. By the following morning they are often fading fast, and within a week no trace of them is visible. Although they appear to be fleeting, they actually come close to holding longevity records for plant life.

The part of the mushrooms ordinarily seen is only its fruiting portion, which springs from the mycelium, a tangled mass of whitish threads lying below the surface of the soil. The same mycelium was mature more than a century ago when the ground above it was shaken by gunfire and rebel yells. When the earth above was soothed by the cooing of thousands of passenger pigeons, interrupted by the sound of the axes felling trees to make way for the farms of the first English settlers, these fragile white threads were vibrant with life. Before that, when only the stealthy tread of the Indian moccasins broke the stillness above, the same mushroom had already begun its subterranean life.

The very origin of the name "mushroom" is lost in the mazes of antiquity. It is thought to be derived from two Welsh words meaning "field" and "knob," but no one is certain. Over the years, legends have grown up about them. Because it was presumed that toads would find them seats of a convenient height, they became known as toadstools. It was commonly supposed that elves found them useful as umbrellas, and, since their poisonous qualities were well known, there were always among the generally accepted ingredients of witches' brews.

The picturesque fairy rings -- perfect circles of tiny mushrooms which often spring up overnight in open fields -- were used as ballrooms by the wee folk as they frolicked through moonlit summer evenings. Any human who stepped inside the fairy circles ran the risk of being bewitched. The scientific explanation for these concentric growths is that the mycelium, which develops from the spores shed by a mushroom, grows outward in a circle. It has been estimated that some rings, measuring more than fifty feet in diameter, are at least four hundred years old.

The mushrooms that grow around here vary widely in shape. Although most of them bear some resemblance to umbrellas, some look like golf balls, others like funnels, bells, stars, coral, oversized raisins, or even a bird's nest complete with eggs. Beech drops and Indian pipes are also members of this plant family, all of which derive their nourishment from other plants.

It is very difficult to detect the difference between toxic varieties, such as those Nero used to rid himself of an entire group of unwelcome banqueters, and others long savored as delicacies. In 1676, Czar Alexis of Russia died sampling an ill-chosen fungus for lunch. Some mushrooms, such as coral and morels, are so distinctively shaped that there can be no mistakes. Others I figure I can do without tasting.

Indian pipes, *Monotropa uniflora*

The largest and oldest trees in our nation are not found in our National Forests, where the harvesting of timber is practiced constantly in all but small areas designated as wilderness. Instead, the few giants we have left are standing in older residential areas.

There are neighbors, longtime residents of the area, who recall the bark of foxes. I once saw a red fox on our land, but have neither seen nor heard one since. In other cases, wildlife has proved very adaptable in surviving near people and their works, so that I discovered a family of muskrats contentedly settled in a very small lake, often muddy and, in summer, covered with shore-to-shore canoes of day campers.

This spring, I saw a muskrat swimming with his mouth filled with fresh greenery. He climbed unhurriedly out on the bank, saw me, stared for a long, disbelieving moment, then dove back into the water. Another of the species never saw me at all, as he swam across the lake, carrying nest-building materials. He dived purposefully beneath an overhanging bank. It was reassuring to know that they were in residence, going about their business.

Among the other creatures who live out their lives fearlessly close to people are raccoons. Several of our neighbors have complained bitterly at the dexterity of the masked marauders, who are capable of removing the lids of garbage cans if they are held in place by anything weaker than a padlock, but we have never had the nocturnal callers on a frequent basis, probably because our garbage can seldom contains any meat scraps, or because it is next to the dogs' yard. Indeed, except for seeing one peering from his hole, high in a hickory tree, we have never seen them around here. It is somewhat surprising that they do not seek out the orange peels and eggshells covered only with a thin layer of leaves in the compost heap.

We have been grateful that some birds have chosen to nest in the houses Britt has constructed, though often not those for whom they were intended. On one occasion, a great crested flycatcher raised a family in a bluebird house, and almost every spring, there is a contest between chickadees, who prefer moss and lichens for nesting materials and bluebirds, who use pine straw. The bluebirds usually prevail, and the chickadees obligingly move to another, uncontested box.

Other birds seem to prefer to nest near human habitation. The cardinals have several times chosen to set up housekeeping in the boxwood just outside the window. The wrens have laid their eggs and raised their young in the garage and the horse-feeding bin. Their diminutive size made it easy for them to scurry beneath the garage doors when they were closed.

The opening of a telephone conversation with my neighbor one day years ago is cherished by all our family. "I found," she said with deep concern, "a sick bird in my yard and naturally I thought of you." With very little hope that we could be of any real help, we rushed to the rescue. Our attempts to save small, not-yet-fully-feathered birds who have fallen from nests or have been abandoned by parents have been generally fruitless. However, the flicker about whom Nancy the neighbor had called seemed almost fully grown. She found it lurching about her lawn, unable to fly or even to walk properly, and fearing that her cat would find it a fetching plaything, she had put it into a box and called for help.

The young flicker seemed remarkably poised when we lifted him into the car for the ride home, and he opened his beak hopefully whenever we came near. As soon as we got home, we introduced him to a congregation of termites who were munching on the underside of a rotting log in the woods. He attacked them with a voracity and speed which demonstrated that, whatever else might ail him, his appetite and his vigor were still intact.

For several weeks, Flicker was content to stay in his shoebox on the porch, except for forays into the woods where he wobbled about finding food for himself. However, he had shown no inclination to try to fly, although we could not see that anything wrong with his wings. Finally, we took to holding him a few feet above the ground and tossing him gently into the air. There was much excitement and rejoicing when he fluttered his wings and coasted to a safe landing. As the days went by, we elevated him inch by inch, and he increased his flights to twenty or thirty feet.

Meanwhile, it was fascinating to be able to observe his spectacular markings at close range -- the black line extending from the sides of his powerful beak, and the black bib placed low on his chest. We admired the bright orange-red splash on the back of his neck, and, best of all, the golden undersides of his wing feather, which reminded me of the solution of a mystery which had puzzled me for several years during my childhood.

One of the pleasures of my youth had come in the collecting of feathers, particularly colorful ones that had been shed by the birds who flew over our backyard. The cardinal, blue jay, and bluebird were the customary donors. Then there came a treasure of a long feather, tan with black markings above and burnished gold beneath. At first I thought it was a gift from the goldfinch, whose pictures I had seen in books, since I knew of no other golden birds. It was several years before I found out that this could not be, for I finally saw a goldfinch pecking away at the zinnias in a neighbor's garden, and realized that this small canary-sized fellow could never have borne a feather of the size of my prize. Later I came across a story in a children's encyclopedia about Goldenshafts, the flicker, and my mystery was solved.

Even though one of his names is "High Hole," our flicker seemed well pleased to browse about the forest floor until we began to suggest urgently that he was supposed to be airborne. When he alighted twenty feet away from his takeoff point, we called encouragement and the children vigorously if ineffectually flapped their arms, but he was content to wait for us to reclaim him and restore him to his shoebox lined with leaves and pine needles.

It was a full month before he soared to a tree and did not return to us. There are many of his species in our woods and we were never certain which of them was our erstwhile invalid. Some years have passed, but only yesterday, as I saw a pair who live in the front woods fly off into the dusk, their white patches above the tails shining like small beacons, I reflected that they seemed less shy than the other birds and wondered if they are our flicker's descendants.

If we never determined what, if anything, was Flicker's physical problem, it was all too clear what ailed the squirrel whom we named Hero. My attention was drawn by a strange shrill cry from the bottom of the five-foot-high rock wall. There lay a half-grown squirrel who had evidently fallen, and although his front legs were frantically active, his rear legs and tail were absolutely motionless.

Although I had no idea whether he could survive, I could not leave him there, so I lifted him carefully and placed him in a box lined with a soft blanket, hoping to ease his final hours. The next morning he was still alive but spurned the nuts we offered. Later in the day his appetite overcame his fear, and he began to eat eagerly. After a couple of days, we put his box out in the dappled sunlight near the spot where we had found him. We watched from the window to see if any parent came to express interest. None did, so the next day we lifted him out of the box and placed him on the lawn. Still no other squirrel came near, but a miraculous thing happened.

Hero, interested in a mushroom sprouting a few inches from his nose, pulled himself forward, using his strong front legs to drag his limp hind legs and tail. He seemed to be in no pain, and having discovered that he could move about, began to do so. We followed, and when he seemed to tire, we retrieved him and put him back in his box, for we feared some predator, perhaps the owls we heard call in the night, would think him tasty.

However, as the days went by and his journeys grew ever longer, we began to consider the possibility that he could eventually be released. There were hundreds of acorns on the forest floor within his reach, and Hero was clearly an independent and even occasionally feisty creature who hungered for his freedom. Each morning we took him from his box and placed him at the edge of the woods. Someone always stood guard, and we watched in admiration as he maneuvered about the ground, finding acorns and hickory nuts, investigating everything in his path. Finally, one day he was accosted by another squirrel of approximately his own size, and they stayed together for quite a while. At last the day we had hoped for and yet simultaneously dreaded came to pass. Hero climbed a tall straight hickory tree. We watched his unmistakable drooping tail vanish into the leafy branches high above. Hero was on his own.

We do hope he survived the owls we heard at night. The little screech owl has a shivery sound, but its far larger cousin, the barred owl, which I saw only once at descending dusk, calls an unmistakable "Who cooks for you? Who cooks for you-all?"

April was considered by the Romans to be dedicated to Venus, and there is a possibility that the name derives from Aphrodite, the Greek name of that goddess of love and beauty. But it seems more plausible, somehow, that April was suggested by the Latin *aperire*, meaning "open," since the buds and blossoms are unfolding at a dizzying pace at this time of year. The glory of the season has always seemed to call for a celebration, and since ancient times the birthday of Rome has been celebrated on the twenty-first of this month. Many features of the Parilia, the Roman festival of herds and flocks, are still observed on St. George's Day, April 23, in Eastern Europe.

Each year, April brings for me a celebration of a feast for the senses, a feast so sumptuous that it leads to frustration. It is simple enough to savor the early spring days, when I can bring to anemone, hepatica, and bloodroot the admiration each deserves when the woods are still bright with sunlight, unhampered by new leaves on trees. During the next few days, the trout lilies' yellow buds will nod, then open to disclose the maroon stamens. Then the dentaria's pink bells rise above its green leaves. The saxifrage sends its delicate white blossoms up above the colorful rosette of red-backed greenery, and still there is time to greet each one.

By later April, though, the crowd scene has begun. The violets, purple, white, or yellow, and the bluets, tiny reflections of the sky in their mossy beds, and the wild geranium all appear.

Wild geranium

Another sense is awakened when the inimitable spicy sweetness of crabapple and pink azalea make the air a delight to breathe. Pink trillium shyly hides its elegant simplicity beneath its three leaves, and there is violet wood sorrel, green and gold, wild borage, the frothy foamflower, and the phlox. All need to be crooned over, and I long to cry out, "Wait! Please wait! Not all at once!" Surely each deserves its solitary moment on the stage.

And all the while, above the flowering of the earth, the darting birds punctuate the sky. Besides the fascination of the nesting business of our usual residents, there come in April the exotic, brief visitors who must be glimpsed quickly or not at all as they fly north for the summer. After many years here, last spring for the first time we saw scarlet tanagers perched in the highest hickory. Even 80 feet above us, the brilliance of their red bodies, contrasting with their black wings, were easily identifiable, even if we had not first heard their distinctive call.

As we walked along the Chattahoochee River one day, we spotted a colorful extravaganza of ten wood ducks perched on a branch, barely above head-height for me. They are the only perching ducks in this country. Perhaps they were socializing before going off in pairs to find nests in the trees near the river.

The palm warbler obligingly fed on the tray just outside the window, so that we could study him at leisure and see the pale yellow under-throat and the russet cap which distinguishes him from other members of his large and confusing family. It was harder to glimpse the swift, tiny blue gray gnatcatcher. The brilliance of the quintet of goldfinches, understandably called "wild canaries," makes them seem like mobile slivers of sunshine as they feast on sunflower seeds.

April is almost too much to experience -- and how I love it!

There is so much to see and hear that it has proved impossible to be aware of everything that happens. A few days ago, Britt called me to come and see a discarded snakeskin, at least four feet long and completely intact. Its owner must have shed it only the day before in the late afternoon or early evening, for the previous morning I'd been harvesting spinach directly in front of where Britt found the skin, and I would have noticed so large a fellow.

We left it where we found it, planning to show it to the children when they came home from school in the afternoon. By then, all that was left was the portion of the skin that had enclosed the head, and another segment about two inches long. Who had taken the rest away? The titmouse, we know, includes a bit of snakeskin in its nest, probably to frighten away predators, but could that nesting couple in the house above the rock wall have used four feet of snakeskin?

When I become annoyed at myself over all that I miss on our four acres, I remind myself of that famous observer, Jean Henri Fabre, who retired from teaching quite early and moved to a small home in Serignan in southwestern France, where for 45 years he studied and wrote about the insect behavior on one small plot of ground.

Luckily, there are other observers in our neighborhood. Stacy, the five-year-old daughter of a friend, noticed a rabbit hopping purposefully toward a small clump of shrubbery. When she followed, she found what I've searched in vain for, a nest of bunny babies. Mama having departed, Stacy lifted one of the very young rabbits, its eyes still closed, from its snug furry nest and carried it home to show her mother. Any authority could have told her that rabbits are so frightened that they die of shock on human contact, but by the time I met this particular rabbit, it was snuggled into a blanket in a laundry basket. Since the young rabbit had never read any authoritative books on the accepted behavior of its species, it made itself completely at home, grew and thrived, and was eventually released into the woods.

Another five-year-old brought home to his mother a flower that any well-informed botanist could have told him did not grow within a hundred miles of here. It was a pink lady's slipper orchid, and it was unmistakable. Incredulously, I followed young Penn to a neighbor's woods, where, in an unusually sandy soil beneath virgin pines, grew literally a hundred of the beauties.

Pink lady's slipper, *Cypripedium acaule*

The owner of the land generously insisted that we transplant several, and they did well for a year or two, then gradually diminished and eventually disappeared. Later, a friend said that the secret was to plant them in six inches of well-rotted pine needles, and this seemed to be the answer, for our second attempt not only survived, but multiplied, until one year when the entire stand was devoured by a rodent of some sort. We have not tried again, but the recent news that the area will soon be sold for development means that we will probably attempt it for the third time.

Crossvine, *Bignonia capreolata*

May

On the morning of May third, the skies were gray, but hardly unduly threatening. Until 3:26 p.m., the only unusual thing that occurred was that an indigo bunting stopped briefly en route from wintering in Cuba or Central America to his breeding ground in New Brunswick or Ontario. I welcomed his startling bright blue hue.

Later, it began to look like rain, so I shut all the windows, leaving only the porch door ajar to bring in fresh air, and I was seated at the kitchen table reading when the door swung open, knocking the lamp to the ground and almost doing the same to me and the chair. I can be specific about the time because all the clocks stopped, and I idiotically went to the picture window to see what was happening. Trees were tossing about frantically, as if trying to escape some invisible force, and there was a sound I thought to be one long uninterrupted roll of thunder. As I gawked, a tall oak uprooted and fell across the garage, and I hoped that the tiny indomitable bunting was well out of range. Later I learned that, in the event of tornado, the thing not to do is stand by a window, but it did me no harm. A larger tree, I learned an hour or so later when it had quieted and I ventured out, had uprooted and fallen across the driveway, dragging down the power and phone wires, and we were embarked on a quiet, powerless, rewarding four days.

The power saw, in sympathy with the other implements rendered useless by the wind, sputtered a couple of times and died when Britt attempted to persuade it to cut the tree barring our use of the driveway, so we got to work with a crosscut saw, and Britt finished up the job with an axe. We were able to cook and indulge ourselves in a warm shower, and for the rest, lit one candle when darkness came at about nine on these daylight-savings lighted evenings. It was a wonderful time, uninterrupted by telephone, television, or radio. We were aware of the turning of the earth as we seldom are when all the appliances are working.

On the fifth day, I heard an unfamiliar, loud bird-call, and, looking up, beheld the wondrous scarlet tanager. He had flown in from South America, and was bound for Quebec or Nova Scotia. It is incredible that so small and apparently fragile a creature can undertake such a journey. It is humbling, too, when I consider how big a deal we will make of traveling to Yellowstone, the Grand Tetons, and Glacier Parks this summer. Would that we had the power to take off, without luggage or food or any means of transportation beyond our own power!

When one has been brought up on Uncle Remus and his tales of little Brer Rabbit outsmarting the fox and the bear, and later graduated to Disney with his adorable small creatures and the threatening predators, who were usually outwitted, it is easy to pay lip service to the belief that the balance of nature is set up for the "bad" critters to survive on the "good" ones, but hard to remain impartial when the drama is played out right before one's eyes.

Britt fashioned the proper-sized hole in a Clorox container to attract a pair of wrens to choose it as a home. Set on a tall cabinet in the garage, it seemed an ideal domicile, and we have enjoyed watching the comings and goings of the perky little brown birds and have loved hearing their surprisingly loud songs. Eggs were laid, and we could tell by the urgent and frequent trips of male and female to the nest that young had been hatched.

Then we found a visitor by the back steps, his head resting on the door sill. It was a four-and-a-half-foot long milk snake, harmless to humans and quite unconcerned by our interested scrutiny. After a while, he slid down the steps and across the turnaround, vanishing unhurriedly into an opening in the concrete by the garage. One of the adult wrens hopped about the concrete, watching the snake constantly until its tail finally disappeared into the crack.

About ten that evening, as we came back to the house from tucking the pups in for the night, we saw one of the young wrens, fully feathered, but not yet large enough to fly, dart quickly across the floor of the garage and scamper toward the garden by the side of the driveway, where a brother or sister had just taken refuge. Looking upward at their former home, we noted that its position had changed and that a long tail hung from its doorway. Balance of nature be damned! While I yelled, Britt grabbed the container and shook it violently. All four-and-a-half feet of the milk snake, which had somehow been coiled inside, hit the concrete with a thud. So far as we could tell, there was no tell-tale bulge to mar its slim lines, and it moved with agility and probably astonishment to seek refuge beneath the pavement. Had it found a young bird for dinner, we are pretty sure it would have been lumpy and lethargic.

The next morning I saw one of the adult wrens darting for his home. It was too dark to search out the wren family by then, but next morning we were reassured to see the parents tending to three young in the woods. We thought it probable that the whole family escaped.

Bluebirds are a puzzle to me. We have built a birdhouse tailored to their very specific requirements, have mounted it, facing southward in the front vegetable garden, and then eagerly waited to see if they would oblige us by taking possession. Last year, after browsing the woods from the first of the year onward, the pair finally determined that only the house on the hill above the back vegetable garden would do, and they were not deterred by the fact that a chickadee couple had already taken possession. They buzzed the place, and on one occasion, I saw the female bluebird enter the dwelling and drive the chickadee out. This year, they have actually settled in and nested where we hoped they would, after a considerable amount of to-ing and fro-ing, and appearing so shy that any entrance of ours into the garden to clear a row for seeds or to plant seemed to threaten them.

Now I would find all this reticence more convincing, had we not, in the past, had bluebirds who doggedly raised a family in the mailbox, seemingly oblivious to the magazines hurled at them daily. There also was the adventurous pair who laid eggs and raised babies in the hollow of a post holding up a tennis net, though the post was metal and actually too hot to touch in the spring sun. Whenever a ball hit the net, the post and its occupants vibrated. This year, I was at first saddened to see what I took to be the limp corpse of a male, sprawled on the railroad crosstie that bounds the garden. It was a cool day, and as I saw him rise, shake himself and fly off, only to return to assume the same unique posture a few minutes later, I concluded that the tie was wondrously warm and soothing, or alternatively, that some trace of creosote remained that was unattractive to its mites.

In mid-May, the ruby-throated hummingbird arrived, fresh and fast after his 500-mile trip across the Gulf of Mexico from his wintering grounds on the Yucatan peninsula. He spurned the coral honeysuckle after a brief sampling and settled down to gorge himself on the purple flowers of the sage.

Deep in the backwoods, Britt spotted a brown nuthatch, much smaller than his more common cousin, the white-breasted nuthatch, but unmistakable as he descended the trunk of the poplar head first. He had nesting material in his beak, but he must have decided on a destination quite near the dead pine log where we sat to observe, for although he flew from tree to tree, coming nearer and nearer, he would not commit himself to a spot. We departed to let him go about his constructive duties in peace.

This year, for the first time, the native holly that miraculously appeared beneath our bedroom window is covered with flowers. Now the bees are happily exploring them, and we wonder which birds will fancy their berries come autumn.

Pasture rose, *Rosa virginiana*

Another premiere this May was the flowering of the delicate pink pasture rose, the only native rose of our region that I know of. We had found a colony of the plants in our deep woods and watched them for several years, but although they liked the area well enough to spread from the roots and enlarge the group each spring, there was not enough sun to make them bloom. We moved a trio up to a sunnier woods area, and they have responded beautifully. My inspiration for the move was a plant of the same variety that blossomed profusely each year at the edge of some woods en route to the garden center where I work. Such observation has proved more valuable to me than any book I've ever found in determining what will grow where.

The spring has been cooler than customary this year, and the mountain laurel are a froth of deeper pink.

Mountain laurel, *Kalmia latifolia*

Its close cousin, the rhododendron, also more at home in the mountains than here in what is technically called the Piedmont region, is flowering away.

Rhododendron nudiflorum

The coral honeysuckle vine, which we transplanted from an area near the river when lumbering activities threatened, has loved its move to a sunnier spot and threatens to engulf the porch in its sprays. On the other side of the porch another native vine, the *Clematis viorna*, which we brought from the same location, is already festooned with its thick lavender bells. I cannot understand why both are not used more often in landscaping, except for the persistent belief, expressed by one horticulturist I know, that "native flowers won't grow here!"

Clematis viorna

Just when I am certain that spring can only bring renewed

acquaintance with the plants I already know from other years as residents, I find something new, which shows that the birds and the wind are constantly at their planting. Just today, by Nancy Creek, a whole colony of partridge berries, which at this time of the year look more like their other name, twinflowers, are covering the bank, and there is watercress in the stream by Crane's lake, in the area now too overgrown to reach, but I make a mental note to visit in early spring next year.

Speaking of edibles, a group of Jerusalem artichokes have sprung up near the holly -- I can hardly wait for a taste. This year I have found that poke really does taste like asparagus when gathered early while the stems are green and tender.

When I first saw the strange behavior of a pair of flickers, I assumed that a large young one was cajoling a parent for food. The bird stood, about four feet from the adult male, wagging its head back and forth rhythmically. However, its beak was not yet open, and when the male bird imitated the motion, and then each bird in turn executed a similar dance step, I decided I was witnessing a courtship ritual. It was a formal set of movements, interrupted only when the female (whom I had mistaken for a young one) vanished behind a bit of shrubbery, then emerged in what was clearly a peek-a-boo routine. They were lost to view when she finally tired of the game and walked toward the deep weeds, with the male following at a respectful five-foot distance.

Other birds have already finished their spring housekeeping. The chickadees occupied two of the houses, having constructed their beautiful and intricate nests entirely of moss. They laid eggs, raised and launched their young. The bluebirds are so wary that we had to vacate the vegetable garden where their house stood in order to allow them to feed their babies. If we stayed, they perched nearby, often with a worm caught in their beaks, but refusing to enter the house, where the babies could be seen at the door eagerly waiting. The titmice had used some moss to build their nest, but had completed the task with synthetic fuzz from the living room rug, thereby vindicating Britt's habit of emptying the vacuum cleaner in the woods. No more will I complain that nylon will stay there forever. The towhees are still feeding their young in the nest in the hedge, complaining loudly whenever we walk near.

June

Usually, by the time June has arrived here in Atlanta, the weather has turned too hot and buggy to take to the woods, where chiggers wait invisibly but infuriatingly. This year, however, it has been wonderfully cool, so I wandered over to see the plants and creatures at the quarry and the waterfall.

This area was the campsite of the Union Army when it first crossed the Chattahoochee River on its way to the Battle of Atlanta, but all signs of its brief tenancy have long ago vanished. An elderly neighbor told me that he recalled seeing fifty or more years ago an ancient beech carved with the date, *July 1864*, but the only tree we could find which showed signs of carving was one which had bears' markings at an impressive height. We have never seen a bear there.

This morning, there was tranquility and the usual variation of plants. The aquatic weeds waded in the shallows of the lake, the arrowhead with its distinctively shaped leaves and its white blossoms...

Arrowhead, *Sagittaria latifolia*

...and purple pickerel weeds, and marsh grasses, while above them the rocky cliffs were home to brilliant red fire pink, as well as the regal white bells of yucca. Although the latter is better known as a desert plant, there are species native to our area. Today, as is most often the case, a very small creek tumbles over the rocks into the lake, but I remember the elemental thrill of watching, with six-year-old son Craig, the effect of a sudden summer storm. It came on far too quickly for us to run home, so we sat on the rocks, soaked and delighted, while the little stream grew to unaccustomed proportions and our small waterfall became a torrent, a real force.

Fire pink, *Silene virginica*

At home in the garden, memories are also blooming. The old-fashioned balsam, or touch-me-not, in shades of pale pink through bright red to maroon, recalls the small shy old couple who clung to their little country house long after the city grew up around it. Whenever I went to the library, I stopped to admire their small, carefully tended flowerbeds. The little old lady was often out, weeding or cutting off dead blossom stems. I stopped to praise the beauty frequently and she nodded, casting her eyes downward beneath her sunbonnet, smiling a very little, but never speaking. I do not know whether she could no longer hear, or whether she simply felt too overwhelmed by the crowds and the noise and the brash large buildings to talk.

One day when I came, the little house had been obliterated, with only baked red clay where it had stood only a week before. I learned that the old man had died, and the old lady had gone away somewhere. I prayed that where she went had a patch of ground where she could plant and nurture beauty, and I moved a few of the Rose of Sharon bushes and the balsam from the border that remained. The bank next door, they told me, needed more parking space.

Balsam

Rose of Sharon, or althea

Both plants have made themselves at home here, producing many offspring, and the purple Rose of Sharon (or althea) have a lovely habit of failing to breed true in color, so that there are, in addition to the lavender hue we brought in, now pink and white as well.

June is so profligate with her growth that it is difficult to come inside long enough to record. I celebrated my birthday this morning, June 17, early while it was still cool enough to be blissful in the garden, by harvesting raspberries, broccoli, turnip greens, and bush beans. We have recently read that the lovely lush heart-shaped green leaves of the sweet potato are prized as an Oriental delicacy.

The vegetable gardens have done well this year, with generous harvests of spinach and lettuce already past, and the customary small crop of sweet early peas. It is really pretty foolish to devote garden space to the latter, but they grow in the otherwise fairly dismal month of February, and this year, they even sprouted in January. It did a lot for my spirits to be able, on a wintry day, to lift the screens, lined with plastic (made from leaf sacks also discarded by neighbors) and see the new fresh growth. Therefore, I guess it hardly matters that we harvested only about nine servings of peas in all.

Some of the most ample harvests have come this year from crops we never planted at all, the watercress from the stream at Rivermeade, the dewberries alongside the road bordering the expressway, and, most of all, the twenty or so quarts of apple sauce in the freezer, which mostly came from a tree on the property of an elderly neighbor. While our own tree bore more fruit than ever before in its young life, our squirrels are more grasping, and we were lucky to glean some bitten ones discarded by the bushy-tailed fellows, plus about two dozen green apples we grabbed early. Meanwhile the tree at the Withers' had two large branches actually break from the weight of the fruit! Some day, we are sure, our tree will grow large enough to provide both for us and our furry friends.

The poke salad has grown and grown and grown, in spite of regular picking. This year, I devised a new way of preparing it that Britt loves. I boil it in two different waters, discarding the supposed poisons (which I do not think exist) with the first water. Then I whip the leaves in the mixer, adding cream and a couple of raw eggs, and bake a casserole at medium heat until the mixture sets. I sprinkle with Parmesan cheese just before serving. Five guests from Montana made pigs of themselves with this concoction last week. They were amazed and delighted to hear they had consumed "poke sallet."

A cultivated camellia, related to the tea plant

July

Of all the creatures who share our land, I find the rabbits most fascinating. Perhaps it is because for many years we rarely saw them, although we knew by the round droppings on the lawn, and by the neatly cropped foliage of the early phlox and the leveling of the crocus that they emerged from the woods in the evenings. Driving home at night, we would occasionally catch them grazing in our headlights. On such occasions, they would stay absolutely immobile. We waited in vain for a glimpse of their cotton tails, for they always outstayed our patience.

Chattahoochee phlox before the rabbits' feast

As the years have gone by, the rabbits have become bolder, and now we can count on their presence in the early mornings, nibbling at the grass, with their enchanting mobile faces, as they chew from side to side, unlike other members of the rodent order that slide their lower jaws front to back. We had a lengthy exhibit of the chewing technique of rabbits when, one morning, we saw a young one nibbling at the thrift, which Britt had encouraged with considerable effort to grow on the rock wall beneath our bedroom window.

At first, we watched fondly and silently while the small bunny munched away, but then as it became clear that this particular fellow had decided that thrift was his very favorite breakfast and had no intention of moving on until its last leaf was devoured, Britt became less quiet. "Go away," he first suggested in a conversational tone, and we expected the shy character to hop in terror. He continued to feast calmly, even as Britt shouted, then scratched on the window screen and made horrid faces. It was clear that only a rush at him would send him in search of grass or clover, and we concluded that the thrift, while undeniably lovely in its pink cascades in early spring, was hardly worth the destruction of the trust we had built up, so we left him to it and went downstairs to our own breakfast.

A few days later, I walked within three feet of a small rabbit, either the glutton or his twin, as he crouched beneath the amsonia in the wild flower garden. He was either frozen in fear or stayed immobile because there was no reason to flee. In any event, I squatted down and admired him, with his smooth brown fur and his shiny alert brown eyes, but I did not speak, and he was still there when I left.

We watched another facet of rabbit life. So far as we had been able to determine from our observation, the creatures spent all their time either eating or browsing about deciding what to eat, but it was quite late -- about nine o'clock on a Sunday morning -- and they must have eaten their fill, for we saw a pair romping. They charged at each other, much like puppies at play, and one leaped, apparently for the pure pleasure of it, straight up in the air when he was about to bump into the other.

The leaper soon found another diversion. He stretched out luxuriously first on his side, and then on his back, exposing his snowy white belly, in a patch of dry dirt beneath the children's swing. He wriggled sensuously, got up, hopped a few feet away, then returned to his dusty play.

His behavior was very similar to that of a pair of thrashers I had watched a few days before. They were taking dust baths in a particular spot where the mud, brought home from a riverbank beneath the car of one of our kayaking sons, had dried. There was only enough room for one bird to spread his wings while lowering himself into the dust, then peck at it and apply it to the areas beneath his wings. It turned out the soil contained mica, whose sharp points were effective at scratching out mites beneath their wings.

What a difference a few feet make! I have wandered and watched the shore of our river, and I thought I knew the area intimately, with the frothy clematis draping trees and shrubs along the shore, and the beauty of spider webs outlined in sparkling dew as the first sun's rays break through the morning mist. But there is another world just beyond, a world best explored by canoe.

Trumpet vine, *Campsis radicans*

A constant panorama of change and beauty flows smoothly by as we paddle upstream. Crowding the riverbank are the brilliant reflections of the first scarlet lobelia, the cardinal flower, the muted likeness of its cousin, the blue lobelia flowering nearby, the large yet delicate heads of the Joe-Pye weeds, the orange bangles of the jewelweed, and the monkey flower, with its distinctive square stem. The trumpet vines festoon the river birches and overhang the water, so that their bell-shaped blossoms drop into the water and are borne southwards.

The Chattahoochee River is a precious commodity, the fresh water which has its beginnings far up in the Blue Ridges, and which flows eventually, after joining forces with the Appalachicola, into the Gulf of Mexico. Only one percent of the earth's surface is covered by fresh water, and this small area is home to fascinating creatures. The silence and the slowness of our approach is reassuring to the muskrat, the beaver, and the birds who will allow us to come very near. A pale green luna moth drowses away the day on an alder branch, while a young blue heron, snowy white at this stage of its development, picks its unhurried way from rock to rock.

This morning, Scott and I see a rare visitor, the American egret. A series of explosions of wood ducks fly across our path, otherwise camouflaged and invisible in the rushes at the shore where they shelter. The brilliant colors of the male during breeding season are muted to dun during the summer.

It has been an unprecedentedly hot and dry summer, so that, during our ten days away in Tennessee, Kentucky, and the North Carolina mountains, the vegetable garden virtually fried and, even in the woods, the dogwood leaves are drooping piteously. But we think it possible that the weather was responsible for one delightful visitor. We have mourned the lack of flying squirrels at this house, having only glimpsed one of the enchanting creatures briefly one night as he "flew" onto the screen of a window upstairs, then vanished almost immediately. Yet a few days ago, as we drove into the garage at six, the hottest time of the day, I felt someone looking at me, so intense was the gaze of the very large dark eyes of the flying squirrel in the birdhouse on the nearby tree. This domicile, originally designed to the specific demands of bluebirds, had long ago had its doorway widened by the teeth of the gray squirrels who occasionally took refuge there during the winter months. This year a titmouse family had raised a brood there, and now evidently a cousin of the gray squirrels had moved in.

How he happened to be awake and curious in the broad daylight we do not know, but we theorize that the heat and his fur coat made it impossible for him to sleep the day away, and that the noise of the car had brought him to the doorway to investigate. At any rate, though we have not glimpsed him again, we know he is nearby, as we know the raccoon, once spotted peering from a hole in a neighboring tree, is in residence, though mostly invisible.

Lycoris

August

It has been encouraging to note that even the most delicate-looking creatures seem able to withstand the merciless sun of this searing summer. The hummingbirds feed at the salvia every morning, and the garden spiders have set up housekeeping by almost every window, waiting in their fascinating webs with the enticing messages writ across, perhaps a written invitation to the prey attracted by the lights in our house.

This summer has been a lesson, too, in the marvelous qualities of compost. The new vegetable garden in the back, whose soil is completely rotted organic matter, has thrived in a jungle-like way, while the old garden, growing in soil only thinly coated with compost, has shriveled. Long live neighbors and their profligate discarding of their leaves and grass clippings!

It has been about five years now since the early summer morning when I was strolling toward our backwoods, enjoying the sparkle of dew on the spider webs, the soft song of the thrushes in the underbrush, and the fresh new green all about me. Suddenly I smelled grape soda for the first time on our land, and I knew, to my horror, that it came from the dreaded kudzu, that rampaging cousin of the green bean, sweet pea and lespedeza.

Kudzu was introduced from Asia to the United States at the Philadelphia Centennial Exhibition in 1876 for use as an ornamental and forage crop. Then well-intentioned agronomists encouraged its use in the South during the 1930s through the 1950s to halt the devastating erosion of our worked-out cotton fields, where deep gullies scarred the red clay. The strong vines, which grew with lightning rapidity, did the job well. The only problem was that their strong vines did not stop at the boundaries of the fields, but leaped enthusiastically to drape themselves over trees, telephone poles, houses, and, it is rumored, over livestock and people who failed to move quickly enough.

After a few years, its advantages were all but forgotten, although we had an elderly friend who claimed that, when she had aggressions to work off, she found a session of struggling with the kudzu that threatened her small cabin left her too exhausted to fret about any issue, however large. Native crafts folks learned to weave the indestructible vines into baskets, and some farmers claimed that it made excellent fodder.

None of these uses were of any comfort to me that morning as I tracked down the vine, small yet, but already stretching its tendrils toward the young dogwood trees. The bunches of flowers, rather similar to wisteria, were quite pretty, and the three-parted leaves were beautiful in design, and I might have savored their appearance had I known that kudzu does not thrive in shade. This invader eventually disappeared from our woods.

The organic discards of our neighbors, gathered in their plastic sacks from the roadsides and added to our copious compost bins, sometimes produce fascinating mystery plants. This year a large fruit developed on the lush vine that sprouted, uninvited but welcome, among the tomatoes. It was a green oval, and we wondered if it were some form of squash, miraculously untouched by the borers which invariably attack all those we plant on purpose. Although we puzzled over it, we could never identify it and did not summon the nerve to taste it.

August has brought, for the past several years, two beautiful floral reminders of the need to appreciate the plants that come unbidden and generally unappreciated. Climbing by the back door were the tangled vines and the gloriously intricate blossoms of *Pasiflora incarnata*, better known as maypops. Having seen them all my life, I'll admit to have come to a proper appreciation of them only during a visit to London.

We had gone to the Chelsea Flower Show, which featured so incredible and varied a display of flowers that I had reeled from one to the other for several hours, rather like a drunken bee, only to be brought up short in speechless admiration at a group of *Digitalis purpurea*, straight and tall, ranging in color from white with barely perceptibly spotted throats, to deepest purple. Behind me, two countrywomen had paused also, but with a different reaction. "Would you look at that?" one asked the other indignantly. "Why, 'tis nought but foxglove!" And they walked briskly away from the plants, found uninvited and unwelcome in many a field throughout England.

Although I said nothing to the women, I was annoyed at their inability to perceive the beauty, and I said so that evening. Next morning, I was unwontedly silent when the *London Times*, a journal noted for its lack of photographs, devoted an entire page to a close-up of a flower brought from America especially for the show -- a maypop.

Maypop, *Passiflora incarnata*

The other plant adorning our garden is downright cursed, for the goldenrod is blamed for hay fever. The real criminal is ragweed, an insignificant plant with small greenish flowers, which blooms and sets its troublesome pollen adrift at the same time that the goldenrod, far showier, is flaunting its plumes.

Goldenrod, *Solidago canadensis*

We have two varieties of goldenrod. The *Solidago canadensis* prefers the regular garden, while the *Solidago altissima* (which means "tallest") selected the gardens on either side of the driveway to spring up, as tall as their name, and, then, as the late summer rains and heaviness of their own heads bowed them, arching with grace. They are glorious flowers, and their color has probably led to the legend that one who carries them will find treasure. Its discovery by the early English explorers led to the export of powder made from the flowers and sold, during Queen Elizabeth's time, for as much as half a crown a pound for its healing powers.

Friends who traveled to the Botanical Gardens in Bangkok, Thailand, brought home reports that they followed arrows pointing to *Solidago canadensis* the entire length of the grounds only to find a wizened single specimen of goldenrod. We now greet both varieties of goldenrod with deference and delight.

Atamasco lily

September

Usually the hottest month of the year here, September seems to be making a beautiful attempt to atone for the hottest summer in fifty-three years. The sky, after several days of rain, is washed to clear October-deep blue, and there is an autumnal crispness in the air.

Goldenrod, asters…

New England asters, *Symphyotrichum novae-angliae*

…blazing star, cardinal lobelia, and its smaller cousin, blue lobelia, are all flowering.

The butterflies seem especially active, as are the bumblebees. More than usual, the mushrooms are brilliantly colored and larger. An exceptionally big succulent puffball tempted me to sauté it with lots of butter, but the result was no more flavorful than before, which isn't very.

My cowlick was almost knocked flat by a low-flying immature green heron, winging in from Nancy Creek to take up his immobile stance on a branch at the shore of the little lake at the Westminster Summer Camp. After the rains, the waters are orange and completely opaque, and in any event, the lake is so small that I would not think it sheltered any fish worth the heron's while. However, he perched there, still as a statue, and quite oblivious of my approach to within five feet or so. There were a couple of surprisingly large splashes but he paid them no mind. He was still there, watching with incredible patience, when I moved on.

Blazing star, *Liatris spicata*

I saw several varieties of fall warblers nearby — I have decided not to spoil the pleasure of watching them by trying to identify the exact species — but several were about the size of juncos, had dark backs and wings, clear lemon-colored undersides, and a rather sedate fight pattern between hickory branches and the ground. A far smaller pair, about chickadee-size, whose wings showed flashes of white as they flew, behaved as if they were besotted with joy, staying very close and performing an aerial ballet. They may have been gnat-catchers, but if so, the hunting was either poor or they gulped their prey too swiftly for my eyes to catch. They flew, turning flips and sweeping in long curves, then returned to their branch.

October

A loud, cawing cacophony brought Britt, Scott, and me outside early in the morning to watch about a hundred of the big black crows wheeling and complaining, following a leader to light in adjacent trees, then rising and circling to shout alarm before lighting again. This went on for about ten minutes, and it was clear that they were mightily disturbed about something, but we could not determine the cause. It seemed unlikely that mountain lions, recently reported to have returned to the Cohutta wilderness in the north of the state, could have wandered so far afield, though my recent sighting of a very small cousin, a bobcat, sunning himself on the rocks near the Chattahoochee, had my mind running in that feline direction.

Then we saw the culprit. Red-shouldered hawks, small indeed in comparison to the crows, were flying over. There were only about five of them, heading south toward the Okefenokee Swamp, their favorite wintering grounds, and they paid no attention whatever to the large flock of crows. After a while the alarm-raisers, lacking any cornfields to plunder, flew away, presumably to feast on the garbage in the parking lot of the supermarket a mile away.

Other travelers, spectacular ones, stopped by to sample the poke berries. They were showy, large rose-breasted grosbeaks, easily identified by the triangle of red beneath the throat. Another seldom-seen species, the crested flycatchers, flew in today. They are glorious, proud birds. Another migrant comes every autumn to visit the eleagnus hedge of a neighbor — a large flock of cedar waxwings.

There is nothing so wonderful to watch as the renaissance of a creek. It is not a sudden or noisy occurrence, but a gradual step-by-step return to life. Nancy Creek never runs dry, but its waters were more often than not rusty red when I first began to observe it on a regular basis about twenty-five years ago. Much building went on upstream, and no attempt was made to save the stream from mudslides where construction denuded the land of every tree, and indeed every blade of grass.

No fish survived in its muddy waters, and the shrubs which did dare to grow along its shores were puny things, sapped of energy by the heavy coat of mud deposited on them whenever a heavy rain swelled the creek.

I do not know whether legislation or simply the fact that every bit of land that could possibly be built on — and some that could not, but was anyway — had been used. In any event, I began to notice that the creek ran red less frequently, and one memorable day, about two years ago, I saw the first minnow! As the fish population gradually increased, and I heard tales of eating-size fish being caught in our vicinity. One morning I heard an unfamiliar bird cry and looked up to see the unmistakable blue-gray and white flash of a kingfisher patrolling above the water.

Gradually the banks have reverted to their original sandy selves and began to record the footprints of visitors. The raccoon came again to soak his dinner, leaving his delicate five-fingered tracks. A small cooter turtle began to spend a good part of his time there before noon, and his parallel tracks looked like a miniature pair of train tracks.

After a few days out of town, I returned to Nancy Creek and read a puzzling message on the sandbank. Some creature had come and peppered the entire exposed area with round markings of varying sizes. Although I examined it carefully, I had no hint of the source of the strange prints; there were no droppings, nor any residual odor from the unaccustomed caller. However, the day's newspaper gave me the solution with its weather report. There had been a fierce hailstorm!

This year, the muscadine vines on the banks have produced a bumper crop of large juicy grapes, and the spires of cardinal lobelia have come to join the golden carpet of Confederate daisies.

Cardinal lobelia, *Lobelia cardinalis*

I am watching for the rings of raised sand that signal that crayfish are here, too, but they have not yet arrived.

November

The chipmunks and squirrels are skittering noisily, and there are other smaller scurrying sounds, perhaps lizards or wood mice, but they do not let me see them. The jays clamor, and the blackbirds squeak, but the wrens and thrushes, continuing their brown searches through the underbrush, are silent now. How fortunate I am that I can walk these miles adjacent to home and seldom see my own species! This morning a couple of yardmen were raking leaves from an ivy-covered hill — I think the leaves are pretty and fitting for November.

There are reminders, of course, that man's hand is everywhere, even by the river, where I was at first surprised to note that the banks were moist, since we are seven inches short of rain this year. Then I remembered that the Chattahoochee rises and falls not according to the rainfall, but according to the opening and closing of the dam upstream. As I watched the water, flowing slowly toward the Gulf, I heard a splash on the far side, as of a large creature seeking its depths, perhaps a muskrat. I could not see, and although I waited a while to see if it would surface, nothing disturbed the barely moving surface of the river.

The very words, mid-November, have a somber sound to them, but today, as I hiked three miles in search of hickory nuts for the orphaned squirrels Scott has adopted and nursed through eye-dropper stage to bottle to voracious gobbling of nuts (but only after they have been gathered and cracked), I saw color and heard much activity in the weeds. True, many of the trees have shed their leaves, and they crackle crisply under foot this dry autumn. The yellow of the hickories and poplars has long gone, as have the reds of sourwood and dogwood, yet the sumac flies its brilliant red flags of defiance at oncoming winter, and the red oaks cling tenaciously to their rich, coppery-maroon foliage.

In addition, there remain, this frostless fall, dandelions, brightly winking at the leaden sky, and the seasonal pink and white camellias with their softer hues. Color is far from gone, and along the banks of the small stream the deep blue of bottle gentians are especially rich this year.

When you have lived in one spot for thirty-five years, what new can you expect to see and hear? A lot. This autumn, an ironweed (*Vernonia noveboracensis* if you are fond of syllables) appeared magically in the weeds quite near the house, flaunting its deep purple clusters of blossom as high as my head with justifiable pride. Whether the wind or birds brought it to share our forest, I do not know.

Ironweed, *Vernonia noveboracensis*

There are new sounds this fall, two great horned owls calling back and forth to each other. At least, it sounds as if they were talking to each other, though Scott says their melodious sounds may be for the purpose of terrifying small prey into seeking a safer refuge, thus exposing themselves to the hunters.

With all the novelties, there is also much that is familiar. The hickory nuts are bursting out of their overcoats. The persimmons are ripening and looking rotten by the time they fall, actually having just reached their peak of mellow goodness, ready to be sieved and baked into a bright orange bread. I learned early and unforgettably not to taste persimmons when they are firm. The mouth puckers almost past return.

As we get ready for the season when dried arrangements must see us through to spring's first blossoms, I am grateful for the foresight of pawlonia, or princess tree, which in early fall sets its buds, sprays of velvety soft brown, which seem to me far more attractive than the large purple, short-lived flowers they will produce in the spring.

Today, since I happened to be standing directly beneath the low small branch on which a red-bellied woodpecker alighted before advancing on the scattered sunflower seeds, I got my first glimpse of the red streak, low on his belly, that gives him his name. It seemed strange that so small and obscurely located a marking could name him, until I discovered that early ornithologists, long before the time of binoculars, collected their birds with guns. Able to study the dead specimen at their leisure, they often named species for markings that are virtually invisible in flight.

Audubon painted his birds using dead models, which accounts for the accuracy of their detail. It would seem strange and awful for birdwatchers to stalk their prey with lethal weapons now, thank goodness, and we can study not only their feathers, but (far more interesting to me), their feeding and nesting habits.

A wren somehow got into the house while I was out. As befits a friendly creature who chooses to nest in such cozy places as mailboxes and horse-feeding troughs, he did not panic. Neither could he seem to find the front door, left wide open for several hours, and fly to the out of doors. He flew from one potted plant to another, investigated, with disastrous results, a bowl of cherry tomatoes left to ripen on the kitchen windowsill, and then disappeared. We finally discovered him, late that night, settled down comfortably for the night in a towel in the laundry room.

We were concerned about his well being, since he had been in the house, away from food, for at least six hours, and we were aware that the metabolism of most birds is so swift as to require almost constant food intake. But after we carefully carried him outside, resting on the towel, he flew off into the crisp clear night quickly, probably settling in the garage, where he or some of his kinsmen have nested for years past. There is no problem of entrance or exit due to the convenient small hole left by the exhaust pipe of a car backed into the garage door. Squirrels quickly enlarged this opening for their own purposes, and now a whole family of wrens could enter, whether the doors are open or not.

That same night we tried new binoculars to scan the sky. The Pleiades were barely visible to the naked eye, but our marvelous new aid not only brought the "seven sisters" nearer, but made clear many smaller stars in the area. Astronomy lies ahead for me.

The juncos came back yesterday and were all clustered about the apple tree. It seems odd that they are called snowbirds. I am told that they have that white breast to camouflage them in the icy stuff, yet every winter thousands of them emulate the human Yankees and head south.
While they attack some insect on the apple tree, a flock of sparrows are busy, as usual, in the raspberry patch. The fruit are long gone at this time of year, except for a few confused berries, and the sparrows seem to have no interest in these. I wonder what does attract them to the bushes.

We continue to scatter seed in the open spaces behind the house, then enjoy watching our customers from the warmth of the library. Yet I am aware that, in order to know our feathered fellows well, I must watch where they feed when there are no handouts. There are a flock of doves, twenty-two at the largest count, who come daily to feed. They must live nearby, yet I have no idea where they nest.

Whenever we canoe the river, there seem to be more varieties of waterfowl. It is probable that I simply cannot make the acquaintance of so many on any one trip. At any rate, this morning I met the coots, and a fascinating family they are, riding low in the water, and looking to my ignorant eyes like ducks. They are not.

They nest in masses of water plants but seem quite amphibious, for their diet includes not only aquatic plants and seeds, but mollusks and an occasional worm. Their feet are superbly adapted to this varied habitat, having fringed toes that make it easy for them to swim or to walk on the ooze where they sometimes venture in search of small reptiles or mice.

The ones I saw were completely black, except for a touch of bare white above their beaks, but I have read that when the ten speckled eggs they lay in spring hatch out, they are colorful creatures, having coats of jet black down on their bodies, with heads of bright startling scarlet.

The tiniest mammal in our area stayed still long enough for me to study it, and there were reasons. The shrew had fallen into the pool, and when we fished it out, it remained quiet for a minute or possibly two, not seeming frightened at ail, but peering at us alertly from bright wee eyes almost hidden in its soft brownish fur. Although it resembles a mouse, it is a member of the *Soricidae* family.

Then almost immediately, it began to dig in the lawn almost frantically, driven by hunger so ravenous that it consumes its own weight every three hours. While it searches for insects and worms, it is protected from larger predators by the possession of a gland in its side from which it can extrude a singularly unpleasant odor. The fact that it has given its name to a vile-tempered woman probably derives from its understandable impatience with any delay in foraging.

There were surprising visitors today. The leaves have for the most part turned brown, the squirrels and the chipmunks are scurrying about searching out the last hickory nuts beneath the fallen ones on the forest floor, and there was a sudden flash of blue outside the window. It turned out to be one of a *menage a trois*, a brilliant male bluebird, seeming even brighter in color against the overcast sky. He and another male and one female are checking out the accommodations at the house above the rock wall, and, incidentally, feasting on the purple pokeberries which hang like jewels on the branches of the largest bush of the species we have ever seen. Tree-size, it towers over the native holly.

Next to the holly and the pokeberry stands a small grove of dogwood whose branches, on this windless morning, are constantly agitated, for the red berries attract first the female purple finch, a rather shabby creature with only the stripes on her breast livening her dun coat, and the bright yellow-breasted warbler. It is harvest time, yet, like the bluebirds, I look toward spring and find promises of its coming in the buds already set on the dogwood, laurel, rhododendron, and azalea.

Dogwood in spring bloom after setting buds the previous November

The activity in the woods is particularly noticeable, as some fallen leaves have opened the vistas, and I can see the white-throated sparrows darting into the brush piles. The steady drumming on the dead pine emanates from a hairy woodpecker.

Frost was late arriving this year, so that, through mid-November, the nicotiana bloomed, while the lantana, tomatoes, and eggplants continued to flower and set fruit. Finally, night before last, it dropped below freezing, and morning found us with ice-rimmed leaves, and a renewed appreciation of what color remained.

The oaks will cling to their coppery leaves through most of the winter, but the bright clear colors of autumn are pretty well gone otherwise. I feel a great gratitude for the bright red of the nandina berries, and for the same brilliant hue of the cardinals, now newly visible in the almost denuded woods. The crest of the pileated woodpecker catches the rays of the setting sun as he hops investigatively about the pile of brush outside the family room window, and the red-bellied woodpecker contrasts with the quieter colors of titmouse and white-throated sparrows who come to feed on the birdseed scattered over the fallen oak trunk.

There is, to be sure, still much green — the hollies, horse sugar, and laurels will stay verdant all winter, and, on the forest floor, the green-and-white of the pipsissewa and the mottled leaves of wild ginger speak of life everlasting, as do the three-parted leaves of the hepatica, which will soon cradle the first buds of spring.

The New England asters are untouched by the cold, and our regular cold-loving gentians are startlingly blue beside the stream, while on our hill, I can admire the delicate green flowers of the pale gentian.

68

Bottle gentian, *Gentiana andrewsii*

December

Our brief southern winter has set in.

In spite of industrialization and pollution, there is one bird which has, relatively recently, spread its habitat amazingly — the red-winged blackbird. According to the bird books, this species abounds in marshes and shores, and it is true that when we traveled to the Georgia coast our first glimpse of these beautiful birds was a sure sign that we were driving over the marshes of Glynn, described by the poet Sidney Lanier as "low-couched along the sea, old chemist, rapt in alchemy."

However, as the years passed, I have become accustomed to seeing red-winged blackbirds far from their original habitat. Their sleight-of-hand change from somber black while perched to the brilliance of their red-orange epaulets when they are in flight can now be seen in the dry fields of Tennessee, and their flocks seem to line the roadsides all the way from Georgia to Vermont. Closer to home, I caught an unfamiliar, puzzling glimpse of them when several of a large flock left the others, who appeared to be snoozing the subfreezing morning away on the hill near the stables, to fly to a tiny island in Nancy Creek. At first they pecked about among the pebbles in an area that is usually submerged. Then they began wading in the frigid water, not appearing to be searching for food, but simply enjoying the icy water.

A few days later I read the account of a pet blackbird, who was discovered, still caged but quite fit, in the debris of an earthquake that had destroyed the Italian village of San Domingo. The bird had survived for two weeks without food or water, and suffered no ill effects. I was not surprised. My observations of blackbirds give me hope that the resilience of some creatures may enable them to survive the environmental poisoning and destruction my species can inflict.

I have learned the same hopeful lesson in observing the succession of plants and animals that have, over a period of ten years, returned to the site of a landslide in the mountains that was at first just a raw red gash of clay. I can still see a difference in the ecosystem from that of its untouched neighboring land. For now, a thicket of blackberries flourishes in the sunlight, and pine seedlings are beginning to grow.

If Britt had not seen the hawk light upon the hickory branch at the edge of the woods, I doubt we would ever have noticed him, although he was large and very close at hand. He perched there for long minutes, only his head moving as he searched the area for breakfast. He was a red-shouldered hawk, and his dignity was immense. We saw him first shortly after we waked on a Sunday morning, and we admired his broad wingspan as he flew to another tree, but although we observed him for nearly half an hour, we never saw him dive on a rodent, which was somewhat surprising, since the leaves crackled constantly as the chipmunks hurried about their errands.

Walking on Old Plantation Road later in the day, I was surprised to see a small flock of doves clustered in a large privet bush. I had never known they liked the blue berries of this common naturalized shrub, and as I came closer I saw that they were enjoying a more colorful repast. There was a bittersweet vine, its brilliant single red berry nestled in its three-parted waxy yellow sepals, and these were the fruit which had drawn the birds. For the first time this year, I've also noticed that bluejays feast on poplar seeds, hopping from branch to branch of the towering trees to peck their find out of the tulip-like chalices.

This past week I've spotted two water-loving birds, a green heron wading at the shore of Cranes' Lake, named for the owners of the property on which it lies rather than for long-legged birds. A hike to the river gave us a glimpse of a duck rising from a pond created by industrious beavers. They have now deserted this spot and moved downstream into what is actually an arm of the river itself, where they have built a series of doomed dams.

This has been a great season for the wild food harvest. There are more than enough hickory nuts for the squirrels and me, so that I have had plenty of goodies to add to carrot cakes and to make pralines. A new ingredient for us this year has been black walnuts. The huge tree that grows between us and the river produced hundreds of nuts from which I have learned patience. It will not do, I've found, to crack them — or try to — soon after they fall, for they are a moist and gooey mess, and they leave virtually indelible yellow stains on the hands. Let them dry for a month or so.

Earlier, I had gathered wild tangy muscadines, which make delicious jam. So do crabapples and blackberries, so that we boast quite a varied assortment. Other harvesters are at work, too. An unhurried opossum comes nightly for the apple cores we put out for him. A raccoon occasionally comes for his share of the loot. Our sunflowers have gone to seed, providing a feast for titmouse, nuthatch, and chickadee. The yellow-bellied sapsucker prefers pokeberries.

Sunflower in full bloom

Sunflower offering seeds

It is usually only in December, when the last of autumn's leaves have lost their color and lie underfoot, when even the late-blooming bottle gentian's blue has faded, that I come to a proper appreciation of fern. In particular, I stop to admire the fresh green fronds of the Christmas fern. Down by the river, the resurrection fern clinging to the branches of the oak are unmistakably alive, even though their leaves were crisp, sere, and to all appearances, totally defunct when I last noticed them in October. Wintry rain has brought them back from the dead – hence their name.

If you want to be a true expert on some form of plant life, and have a limited amount of time and memory, concentrate on fern. Worldwide, there are more than 300,000 species of seed-bearing plants, but only 10,000 fern. Closer to home, there are only about one hundred species in the United States. However, there are surprising newcomers who appear hereabouts, for the spores of fern are so tiny and light that they may be considered a normal ingredient of atmospheric dust. They must drift effortlessly over the Atlantic, for more than half of our native species are also indigenous to Western Europe. The lifespan of spores varies greatly with the species of fern. They may remain viable for years and seem impervious to drastic climatic changes. Germination can vary from a few weeks for *Osmunda* to fifteen to twenty years for some *Lycopodium* species.

When a fern native to Asia suddenly appeared for the first time in Boulder, Colorado, it seemed likely that the spores were brought over the Pacific Ocean to the Rockies by the jet stream. It may not have taken too long, either, since that stream has been known to reach a speed of 400 miles per hour. It was a beautiful surprise for me, before I knew of the peripatetic tendencies of fern spores, to find an unusual delicately-fronded fern growing beneath a white pine brought from the Blue Ridge Mountains by a neighbor. It is a climbing fern, and it has made itself at home in a planter on the coffee table.

More customary dwellers in the woods of Piedmont Georgia are, beside the Christmas and resurrection ferns mentioned earlier, cinnamon, maidenhair and bracken. The last-named three are not evergreen.

Cinnamon fern, *Osmunda cinnamomea*

If a bird's song is a statement of territoriality, we think we can understand why the mockingbird has so varied a repertoire. He is a fierce and effective defender of his turf, asserting so overwhelming a domain over the bird-feeder that we took to scattering seed on the ground beneath.   The mockingbird, after filling his own needs, simply posts himself atop the feeder, frightening away all other comers. He does not seem to have any weapon other than his sublime self-assurance, but that suffices.

Today we witnessed a spectacular example of his bullying talent. A large flock of blackbirds have been in our woods for several days, and when they descended this morning on a dogwood and began to feast on its red berries, our mockingbird quickly dispersed the entire flock. He used no physical force, and he is far smaller than they are, but they all flew off and left him undisputed lord. The blackbirds did not abandon the area entirely, and we could see, in more distant trees, the sunlight gleaming on their glossy reflective blue heads and necks.

The pecking order is mysterious to us. A neighbor tells of hearing jays creating so mighty a ruckus that her attention was directed to their circling and screaming about a hollow high in a tree. It was impossible to determine the cause of their behavior until she trained binoculars on the hole and saw a large black rat snake emerging. They are amazingly good climbers. In the face of the jay fury, he retreated into his refuge. Later observation revealed that the hole was his home, and, on sunny days, when the jays were engaged elsewhere, he often lay stretched full length on the branch above. He shed his skin there, and it fell to the ground, where our neighbor retrieved and measured it at just over four feet.

This neighbor later saw a pileated woodpecker – big enough to tackle just about anything – vigorously pulling a snake from a hole high in a pine tree. The snake fled quickly rather than risk a very long fall. Perhaps that was the same black rat snake I later saw coiled in the back garden, where a flock of crows harassed it until it disappeared into a crack in the rock wall, no doubt complaining that it could find no peace anywhere!

I am a self-proclaimed naturalist, but then there is no other kind. Naturalism, which I'd define as the ability to perceive and appreciate the world, to study its component parts, and to find one's own place, would probably include the study of botany, ecology, geology, astronomy, and archeology, for a start. Our educational system, which offers degrees and advanced degrees in communication, recreation, law, and history, among a hundred other disciplines, does not offer naturalism. It does not really matter, since most of what is needed must be seen, heard, smelled, and touched, not read about or heard in lecture halls.

The lack of encouragement within our formal educational system to pursue such knowledge seems consistent with certain other aberrations of our culture. Allow me, since the end of the year is approaching, to go on a brief rant. According to the morning paper, truck drivers are killing other truck drivers because some want to strike until there are lower fuel costs and others want to drive their trucks. It is very simple to obtain guns or other murderous devices, and so thousands of people kill, usually with guns, thousands of other people every year, and the newspaper hardly takes notice. The truck drivers' behavior is worthy of newsprint because their actions affect our food supply, since most of vegetables and fruits and meats are hauled hundreds of miles from where they are grown to their markets.

In the unlikely event that lower fuel costs could be obtained, there would still be food problems down the road, because forty percent of the nation's vegetables are grown in the San Joaquin Valley in California, where land must be irrigated. The water for the irrigation is turning salty, and the costly mode of alleviating the problem involves killing more rivers, so the folks who live near the rivers depend upon the fish for a living are kicking up a fuss.

We have many acres of land suitable for agriculture right here in Georgia, land that does not need constant artificial watering, nor require the use of hundreds of gallons of gas to reach the market. Yet the food is not grown there. I do not understand this, nor do I understand why, when many of our people are cold in winter and hungry all year round, we spend our taxes on the purchase of deadly weapons, even though we already have enough of these to annihilate everyone in the world many times over.

We know that fossil fuels for energy are running low, and that they are irreplaceable, so we talk a lot about conserving them. At the same time, our utility companies continue to offer lower rates to those who consume most, and we go right on developing such products as electric combs, electric toothbrushes, electric shoe polishers, electric footbaths, and electric deep fat fryers, and people go right on buying them. None of this makes any sense to me, and I am pretty sure that our whole system will come to a grinding halt not too long from now. Meanwhile I shall keep on looking, listening, smelling, and touching the plants, animals, rocks, and waters, none of which worry at all about man and his foibles. There, that's the end of my rant.

Winter has never been my time of year. It has been a season to be endured through concentration on the dogwood, mountain laurel, and peach buds, already set and promising an eventual spring. It has been a time for poring over seed catalogs and gardening magazines and dreaming impossible dreams.

Only the fact that Curran the Great Dane was insistently eager to go for his daily hike hauled me out this morning. In order to get back in time for work at the Garden Center by ten, we walked early, and I'll admit to viewing the frosty scene with misery.

I recall that peaches must have a certain number of freezing hours each year in order to produce the succulent goodness of summer, but I selfishly wish something else would happen now. We approached a field where only a few weeks ago, the golden plumes of goldenrod stood proud. Now the same plumes, grayed and bent by the frost, seemed to mourn.

And yet, as we entered the field, there was a sudden burst of life. A large flock of sparrows, interrupted at their breakfasting on the seeds of the dead weeds, flew in unison, graceful silhouettes against the deep blue-sky. Life is here, always.

I vowed yet again to perceive and savor what is here now, and later in the day, I looked long at the brilliance of the sunlight on the red leaves of the oak.

This day after Christmas was a fine one for a hike. The sky was a deep and unclouded blue, and so were the wings of the bird who flew across the Westminster campus. Two drab female bluebirds followed in his wake, alighting on either side of him in the field. I predict that he will have an interesting spring.

It has been a mild winter to date. Although there have been several subfreezing days and nights, such tender greens as catnip remain untouched, a dandelion shone brightly from the grass. I found two four-leafed clovers and a bud on the Christmas rose in a neighbor's yard.

The purple finch has joined the crowd in the woods beneath Scott's window, and it seems downright unfair that his mate should be so plain. The rest of the wintry residents are busy sharing the sunflower seeds — juncos, nuthatches, titmice, chickadees, doves and thrashers gleaning on the ground, bluejays feeding either from the pots hung on the low branches of trees or from the earth. So long as they get more than their share, they are agreeable. Wrens and sparrows skitter along the garden paths, and towhees take shelter in the hollies.

There was a tragedy the other day, when son Craig observed a hawk fly into a tree and die there. Urged by the discoverer to retrieve it, Britt obligingly erected our tallest ladder and climbed 40 feet up to bring down the Cooper's hawk. Our three youngest offspring each posed proudly holding the prey. After that. I proudly offered it to the mother of a budding taxidermist, who had earlier requested the body of a beautiful indigo bunting that had flown into our picture window.

The mother vehemently declined the hawk. "That bunting!" she sputtered. "It is still wrapped in butcher paper in the freezer, and I can't count the number of times I've run low on food, rediscovered that package, hauled it out and unwrapped that damned bunting. If I did the same with the hawk, I'd think I had a turkey."

On another occasion when a large bird flew against our window, I gained a pleasant if undeserved reputation as an ornithological expert. The children called to show me the dazed bird and asked what kind it was. I had never seen one like it before, and I hedged. "Well, it certainly has knocked itself cuckoo," sending a son to the bird book, where he found that it was a yellow-billed cuckoo. The bird shook its head groggily for a few seconds, then flew away unharmed.

Christmas brought a delightful book from son Mark. It is called *The Beginning Naturalist*, written by Gale Lawrence, whom I envy. She has the ability to put her encounters with nature into fifty-two neat short chapters, one for each week, whereas I find it impossible to organize the world as I see it. I began this journal with the thought that I could write about birds in one section, trees in another, insects in a third, plants in a fourth, etc. Nature, in all her blessed variety and interrelations, completely undoes any hope of such.

Birds live in trees and eat various seeds and insects, so how to classify one subject that encircles three others? I gave it up and continued to keep a disorganized joyous journal. My monthly chronology is at least a token way of organizing my observations.

Gale Lawrence writes that the seemingly futile pecking at bare wintry trees by the titmice and the black-capped chickadees are probably very nourishing. Many of the insects that disappear from view during the winter have not died or fled to a warmer region, as I had always supposed. They have instead gone into a state of suspended animation called diapause, when their vital processes slow down to a rate far slower than those of mammals, and when they take refuge in the bark of trees or beneath the leafy litter of the forest floor, or in the soil. Here they are often sought and found by hungry birds, or eaten by shrews and moles who prowl the leaves.

This year is drawing to its end, and I ponder the artificial way that humans insist on measuring time. There must be some such organization, yet beginning a new year ten days after the winter solstice seems a poor choice. I'm not original in questioning this. The British only got around to celebrating the changing of a year in January a couple of hundred years ago. Until then, they celebrated the year's beginning on March 25, when primroses and violets were popping up everywhere and the world was clearly beginning anew.

Confederate violets, *Viola sororia f. priceana*

Wood violet, *Viola sororia*

People have been squabbling over the months and where they should fall since the dawn of history. Early humans notched a stick or knotted a cord once a day to mark the passage of time. They watched the changing position of the sun and the stars, the phases of the moon, or the habits of plants and animals, so that the South American tribes expected spring when the Pleiades arose. In North America, Indians planted corn when the buds of oak were the size of a squirrel's ear, and the Greek poet Hesiod warned against digging in the vineyards after snails had climbed the plants.

All in all, I'm inclined to think timekeeping went along more smoothly and logically before people tried to maintain it. By the time of Julius Caesar, the Roman calendar, which used the moon as a general guide and left the details of bookkeeping to high priests, was a mess. It had been the priests' task to inform the people when each month began, and when to expect the first quarter of the moon, but from different priests had come different reckonings. As a result, summer months were falling in springtime and were getting earlier every year.

Julius Caesar added February 29 to every fourth year, a system which led to the Julian calendar, which worked pretty well for several centuries. But since the calendar year was longer than the year of the natural seasons, anniversaries began coming earlier and earlier. By 1582 the vernal equinox was arriving on March 11 instead of ten days later. At this point, Pope Gregory XII dropped 10 days from the calendar and decreed that the day of October 4, 1582 should be October 15, and that three times every four hundred years, the leap year arrangement should be omitted.

It was very forward-looking of him to work all this out, and most of the world, after some initial foot-dragging, has gone along. I would certainly have no alternative mathematical procedure to offer, but I know that in the real world, life springs eternal, regardless of what order humans may attempt to impose. I shall try, as its patterns of growth, decay, and regrowth move steadily forward, to obey the suggestion of Michel de Montaigne, made around the same time as Gregory's calendar-fixing: "Let us a little permit Nature to take her own way; she better understands her own affairs than we."

78

Nan Pendergrast in her front garden...

picking flowers for Quaker meeting

Flying in My Mind

Now that I am in my 90th year, my wanderlust has diminished. For many years, the longing to see faraway places was almost painful. It has now given way to an intense gratitude for the privilege of welcoming the arrival of spring for more than a half century outside this same kitchen window. Yet my memories of adventurous years of discovery are vividly detailed, if somewhat cloudy as to precise years. My flights now are not on airplanes but in my imagination, remembering all the birds I have seen on my travels.

Let me begin small with our search for puffins, colorful birds who live thousands of miles from our native Georgia. We were exploring the Gaspé Peninsula and had been promised we would spot many puffins after embarking on a brief boat trip to a nearby small island. But the wind rose too briskly that morning, and we had to move on, puffinless. Several years later, and a continent westward, we finally found the horned puffin, very similar to its East Coast cousin. Easily identifiable by its oversized bright orange bill, it winters at sea, and a few especially hardy members of the flock venture as far south as the Los Angeles area.

A golden eagle surprised us as we sat on a cliff overlooking the western side of Grand Manan Island in New Brunswick. He flew from the shore beneath us, breathtakingly large -- about seven-and-a-half feet across in wingspan. The eagle was evidently as startled by the encounter as we were, for he dove downward. We rushed across the island to report to the park supervisor. He was not astonished and matter-of-factly said, "You'll also often see bald eagles over on this eastern side of the island." But he was amazed when we reported sighting a small flock of cedar waxwings while coming his way. He said that, in his fifteen years on Grand Manan, he had never seen one.

Our sighting of bald eagles was considerably closer to home and was planned. We spent the night at the lodge at Guntersville, Alabama, and rose in the wintry dawn to view about eight of the birds as they flew to Lake Gunter for breakfast. Two of our neighbors in Atlanta have seen an immature bald eagle in their yards, one flying away with a squirrel firmly grasped in its rapacious claws, after mantling it (spreading its wings over its prey) in the woods near her driveway. There are reports of similar sightings in all of Georgia's 159 counties, proof that the banning of DDT saved the eagles from the looming extinction of which Rachel Carson warned us in her book, *Silent Spring.*

Before I married Britt back in March 1940, I was completely ignorant of birds, having instead concentrated, almost to the point of fanaticism, on getting to know every native flowering plant in the Georgia piedmont. On our honeymoon to Middleton Gardens in South Carolina, Britt introduced me to the incredible beauty of a cerulean warbler, who stayed obligingly nearby and immobile. It was the beginning of a lifelong love affair with the miraculous winged creatures. Their migrations of thousands of miles, their infinite variety of shape and color and sound -- all enchant me.

A brief stay at State College, Pennsylvania, brought my first (and last) glimpse of Baltimore orioles -- also known as Northern orioles – with their brilliant contrasting orange and black and their intricate nests.

Earlier, I wrote about my first sighting of pileated woodpeckers and calling Britt at work in panic to ask what they were. Their range, I can now testify from personal encounters, stretches at least from Sapelo Island, off Georgia's southernmost coast, to Vancouver Island, off British Columbia.

A trip to Waterton Lakes National Park in the Canadian Rockies and a hike beside a clear shallow stream brought an incredible discovery. We saw a bird walking beneath the flowing water, stopping to peck at pebbles for sustenance. It was an ouzel, member of a family known as dippers.

We had already been surprised and shoved aside from our path by three bighorn sheep who went purposefully on their way. They were not deterred, evidently, by a sign that turned us back: "Path Closed. Grizzly Bear Territory." When we returned to our parking lot, we were greeted by seven bighorn sheep who were investigating the garbage cans.

When we journeyed to Costa Rica with a group of Quakers in 1990, we were especially eager to pay tribute to a valiant band of Friends who had chosen this destination because the Costa Rican government had made the decision to have no army. The four families, whose heads had just completed prison terms for the crime of refusing to fight in World War II, purchased virtually inaccessible acreage which they named Monteverde (Green Mountains). Original plans to establish a dairy farm proved impossible because of the difficulty of delivering milk to customers, but, with dogged determination, they were able to supply cheese to most of Costa Rica, using oxcarts for the transportation of their product.

The cloud forest, where the pioneers settled, is a region of incredible richness and beauty, containing 205 species of mammals. 849 species of birds, 130 types of freshwater fish, 9,000 species of vascular plants, almost four per cent of the totals found in the whole world! Obviously it would be impossible to list them all here, but it is worth noting that the first two completely unfamiliar flowers were *Justicia* and *Hysterica*, a combination which seemed to me to have distinctly profane possibilities. On a six-mile hike through the forest, we saw a pair of quetzals, large brilliant green birds with six-foot tails, and a bluetailed mot-mot.

A huge hummingbird feeder mounted in the center of the village of Monteverde attracted constant and varied customers. The purple hummers and their apricot-colored cousins seemed impossible to us, since our feeder at home serves only the ruby-throated members of the family, who are extremely territorial by nature. It is downright frustrating to watch the males, far smaller than their mates, perch for hours on an overhanging branch of the holly tree, only to swoop down to chase away any hummers who have the audacity to attempt to get a sip of nectar.

The Quakers have given a considerable amount of acreage to the nation of Costa Rica with the provision that it always be maintained in its natural glory. The forest now encompasses 35,000 acres.

Another time, in Norway, near Lillehammer, we heard a member of the cuckoo family call repeatedly, sounding exactly like the clock in our house. We didn't ever see him, just as we never saw the bellbird calling melodiously from nearby bushes in New Zealand.

In Maine, we had gone canoeing one early morning, having been promised by our bed and breakfast hostess a sighting of moose. Those huge, ungainly creatures must have slept in, but we were instead startled by a loon who surfaced directly in front of our small craft.

Probably no bird appearance has been more amazing to me than the brilliantly multicolored western tanager that joined us while we ate a picnic lunch on a desolate sandy area in Wyoming. On the entire dismal, treeless journey, driving south from the Grand Tetons toward Salt Lake City, we had gone from the glorious mountain to (in my mind) disastrous desert. During the day, we paused to see Fossil Butte National Monument, which was closed. We found nothing green en route and nothing alive. One bloated deer carcass by the roadside served to intensify my grumbling. It is a wonder Britt resisted the impulse to toss me out of the car.

The chickadees, nuthatches, cardinals, wrens, and jays in our yard seem like members of the family, but it would never occur to any of them to approach within touching distance. I was consequently awestruck to see a chaffinch fly up to perch on the shoulder of the curator of a small museum in Keswick in the north of England. Likewise, we greeted with wonder the flock of sparrow-like birds who came confidently to share our crackers in the forest above Schönbrunn Castle outside Vienna. I wondered if their ancestors might not have been equally friendly to the girl princess Marie Antoinette, while she and her sixteen siblings frolicked there.

Sometimes it is thrilling to be ignorant. I once saw a flock of white pelicans in the Yellowstone River, when I was mistakenly certain that they were tropical birds.

There is no lovelier sound than that the "burgling" sung by flocks of sandhill cranes flying so high as to be nearly invisible on their over-flights to and from the coast each spring and autumn. We could always find them settled in the Okefenokee Swamp, surprisingly tall, gawky, and red-headed, when they appear to be pure silver in the sky.

West Point Lake in Georgia, near Alabama, offered our first glimpse of ospreys nesting on platforms especially constructed for them in the water. From these they dive head first, then turn abruptly to grab fish tail first. Their call is a loud whistle.

We once spotted a prothonotary warbler on Georgia's coast, which was of particular interest because this bird played a vital part in trapping the spy, Alger Hiss. Damn Whitaker Chambers, anyway!

In Arizona, we saw road runners who ran in groups along the roads with their headgear bouncing perkily.

While paddling the crystal clear Ichetucknee River in north Florida from its origin in a spring to its mouth, only about five miles downstream where it enters the Santa Fe River, we were fascinated to watch anhingas fall headfirst into the water, while immobile otters observed.

A six-day cruise, under the auspices of the World Wildlife Fund, brought our first glimpse of blue-footed boobies in the bay bordering the Baja California Peninsula. Here we also watched the greatest activity the natural world ever showed us — a feeding frenzy of dozens of sea birds gorging themselves on a large school of fishes surfacing in an attempt to avoid larger predators beneath.

In contrast, in the village of Rust in Austria, we saw the serenity of storks nesting on every chimney. They were resting, we thought, in preparation for their winter migration to Africa.

From my earliest memories, I have been fascinated with flight, and over all the years, my most fortunate dreams have dealt with my discovery that I could fly, if I spread my arms in the proper position and ran in circles. It was incredibly delightful, and my joy was intensified by the skepticism of an audience, all certain that I would never get off the ground. Sometimes, after quite a few circular runs were ineffective, I too doubted. Yet in these dreams, I always finally soared, no higher than treetop summits but nonetheless glorious.

My only attempt to fly while awake was a childhood leap from the garage roof to the backyard, which landed me, fortunately, in a pile of leaves.

After that, I have settled for the observation of those miraculous creatures, birds. This has brought me wonder in many places of beauty, and I am forever grateful.

Nan Pendergrast
November 2009

Nan Pendergrast holds a six-leaf clover she found

LaVergne, TN USA
10 November 2010
204361LV00005B